INDIA

RICK STEIN'S
INDIA

BOOKS

This book is dedicated to Ed, Jack and Charlie and Sas, Zach and Olive

This book is published to accompany the television series entitled *Rick Stein's Indian Odyssey*, first broadcast on BBC Two in 2013.

The series was produced for BBC Television by Denham Productions
Producer and director: David Pritchard
Associate producer: Arezoo Farahzad
Executive producer for the BBC: Tanya Shaw

10 9

First published in 2013 by BBC Books,
an imprint of Ebury Publishing
A Random House Group Company

The Random House Group Limited
Reg. No. 954009

Addresses for companies within the Random House Group can be found at www.randomhouse.co.uk

A CIP catalogue record for this book is available from the British Library.

ISBN: 978 1 849 90578 7

The Random House Group Limited supports the Forest Stewardship Council® (FSC®), the leading international forest-certification organization. Our books carrying the FSC label are printed on FSC®-certified paper. FSC is the only forest-certification scheme supported by the leading environmental organizations, including Greenpeace. Our paper procurement policy can be found at www.randomhouse.co.uk/environment

MIX
Paper from responsible sources
FSC® C016897

Commissioning editor: Muna Reyal
Project editor: Mari Roberts
Assistant editor: Joe Cottington
Recipe editor: Louisa Carter
Design and art direction: Smith & Gilmour
Photographer: James Murphy
Food stylist: Aya Nishimura
Assistant food stylist: Xenia von Oswald
Prop stylist: Penny Markham
Henna artist: Riffat Bahar

Colour origination by AltaImage, London
Printed and bound in the UK by Butler Tanner and Dennis Ltd

To buy books by your favourite authors and register for offers visit www.randomhouse.co.uk

INTRODUCTION 7

DHABA

…are street snacks the most irresistible food in India? 15

SABZI

…succulent vegetable dishes, transformed by spice 53

MACCHI

…the incomparable taste of fish and shellfish, coconut, tomato, tamarind and spice 121

MURGH

…spicy and creamy chicken curries, fragrant rice dishes and a little roast duck 187

GOSHT

…deep and dark meat curries, kormas, pulaos and biryanis 225

MEETHA

…kulfi, nimish and some other indulgent Indian sweets 279

EXTRAS 303
INGREDIENTS & TECHNIQUES 309
SUPPLIERS 314
USEFUL EQUIPMENT 315
ACKNOWLEDGEMENTS 315
INDEX 316

RICK STEIN
5
Contents

INTRODUCTION

Whenever I hear the word 'curry', I'm filled with a longing for spicy hot food with the fragrance of cumin, cloves and cinnamon. I see deep-red colours from lots of Kashmiri chillies tinged with a suggestion of yellow from turmeric. I think of the tandoor oven, and slightly scorched naan shining with ghee and garlic; of a bowl of dark dal to assuage the heat of the curry, a green chutney of coriander and mint, and a plate with a few tomatoes, cucumbers and sliced onions tinged with pink, all sprinkled with salt and fresh lime juice. At home I have a little sign I put on the front door of my cottage in Padstow which says, *Gone Swimming*. Maybe I'll get one which says, *Gone for a Curry*. The sense of leaving home for something completely satisfying is the same.

The sign would have been there for quite a time while I went for a curry or two in India to make the TV series that accompanies this book. About three months in total, give or take a couple of trips to Australia in between ...

WHAT IS A CURRY?

I wanted to find the perfect curry. I did some research on the subject before I left and began to think that my quest might be fruitless as the Indians don't really understand what we mean by 'curry'; that it's a word to describe the British Raj's rather second-rate interpretation of Indian cuisine. I was also told that the sort of Anglo-Indian cooking that was part of my upbringing – dishes like

kedgeree, mulligatawny soup and beef curry with sultanas and desiccated coconut – were anathema to the Indians.

But when I got to India, I realized that curry was just as much part of their vernacular as ours. It's more specific to them, but they knew perfectly well what we meant. To them, it means a dish with lots of what they call 'gravy', and what we would call a sauce, made with a masala – a combination of ground spices and vegetables, such as onion, garlic and ginger with turmeric, chilli and, more often than not, coriander, cumin, cardamom, cloves, cinnamon, black peppercorns and nutmeg, with liquid in the form of water, tomatoes, ghee or yogurt, and, in the south, coconut milk.

They well understood our use of the word, too, as little more than a generic name for the food of the Indian subcontinent. They had little to say about Anglo-Indian cuisine, because these days it doesn't exist, except in pockets like the old colonial Madras Club in Chennai. But if they do remember those old dishes, it's with nostalgia for places like the station restaurants in the 1950s and 1960s, part of a railway system created by the British. It would certainly not be with any disdain about how awful it was, apart, that is, from curry powder, which was described to me as 'absolutely horrendous', but that would have been a peculiarity of Indian food in England.

Curry, therefore, is a word that, to me, very broadly describes all of the cooking of the subcontinent. A true curry would be something like the egg curry from Calcutta on page 104 or the rogan josh on page 258. But I wouldn't want to exclude the spicy dry-roasted red meat and fish from the tandoor oven or the myriad of deep-fried puffs of battered vegetables, fish and meat, the pakoras, the samosas, prawn fritters. I'd even call smooth, slightly spicy dals flavoured with curry leaves or mustard seeds or turmeric or tomato a curry. Even the glorious rice dishes: biryani and pulao, flavoured with meat, seafood or vegetables with saffron and rosewater.

The search for a perfect curry was a quest to understand Indian food in all its complexities. Why some spices are essential in some dishes, when they are added and how to cook them; how the principles of Ayurveda, the ancient Hindu system for health and harmony in life, underlie so much of the food culture in India. How the food of the Persians with their love of robust meat dishes has overlaid the traditional vegetarian food of the Hindus. It was also about understanding the Indian respect for and sense of comfort from home cooking. I wanted to travel everywhere for dishes deeply flavoured with chilli and spice, a delight to the eye in their rich colours, to understand this fascinating country. Because when Indians talk of food they talk of their life.

In the Western world, we enjoy delicately flavoured food; the Indians, unless they know Europe well, think of it as bland. Many Indians regard Chinese food as equally lacking in flavour, which is why, in India, Chinese food is much more spicy. So why is it that curry is now our country's favourite food? Is there a natural progression from our mother's milk to vindaloo? I joke, of course, but we are

moving towards ever spicier food. I keep hearing people say they are addicted to chilli. Or, are we lucky in the West, that we are privileged to visit such exciting countries as India, to absolutely love the colour and spice, the aromas and robust flavours of Indian cooking, while at the same time also loving the profound greenness of the first asparagus of the season with just a little butter, or a herring caught on an autumn spring tide in the bays of north Cornwall or Devon and simply grilled?

The fact is that the cooking of India is of such colour and flavour it demands our response. Just like the country – you cannot walk down a street there without being aware of an assault on the senses: the heat, the dust, the beggars, the slums, the poverty, the sheer pressure of people everywhere, and yet also the riot of colour, the friendship of everyone, the feeling wherever you go that in spite of the appalling problems of this vast country, you never really feel threatened by anyone. And, in the end, a realization that you can't change anything so you might as well celebrate what you find to love, because there is so much to love in India.

My greatest dilemma in my journey and in writing this book has been that I just don't know enough about Indian cooking, and the more I learn, the more I realize I need to know. So at this stage I'm holding my hands up and saying to any Indian readers, I know there are things in here you won't agree with, but then you don't even agree from one side of Kerala to the other as to what constitutes a proper thoran vegetable curry. I'm no expert, but this is my book and I've done my best to understand a cuisine I love. Here are a few random thoughts on some things I think I might have got right.

COOKING A CURRY

The spice you use must be the best you can find. All Indians say this is absolutely fundamental even though, sometimes, they don't actually stick to it. For example, a good biryani must be made with saffron but hardly ever is – it's usually just yellow food colouring. It is vital, they say, to buy the best and freshest spices you can. If possible, and I know it's asking a lot, buy whole spices and grind them yourself. But feel free, too, to make life a bit easier for yourself and buy ready-ground ones, only make sure you use them well before their shelf life is up. A revelation to me was visiting a spice wholesaler in Cochin in Kerala. He was the grumpiest person I've met for a long time but his spices were magnificent. There were three grades of green cardamoms, for example, so you could instantly see what constituted the best (greenness and size). I picked up a handful of cloves of a perfume I have never before experienced; fabulous, big quills of cinnamon; nutmegs still in their outer casing of mace; ginger and turmeric you could tell had only just been dried and powdered. He was very disgruntled about us filming. Our fixer said that a modest purchase would sort him out, which turned out to be a kilo of each spice. Though I did plenty of cooking in Kerala, we left much of it behind with a heavy heart.

Many curries contain onions; they have to be cooked correctly, which means that they have to be fried in ghee or oil on a moderate heat for at least 10 minutes. (See page 312 for more on cooking onions.)

The order of adding spice in a curry is simple but important. More often than not, a dish will begin with what is called tempering, the first stage of flavouring: whole spices such as cardamom, cinnamon, cloves, coriander and mustard seeds are added to hot oil in a pan and cooked for 30–60 seconds to infuse the oil with their flavour. After this onions and/or ginger and garlic are added, and then the ground spices, most notably turmeric and chilli powder. Great care has to be taken at this stage, and before any liquid is put in, that these are only heated and not burned. One tip I learnt was to keep a little jug of water handy when making a curry. It comes in very useful, particularly at this point, because if there is any danger of burning the spice, pouring in some water will prevent it. After the ground spices have been added, then the wet element will follow – tomato, yogurt, water, tamarind. If it's a meat or poultry dish, this will normally go in with the ground spices; very rarely is it browned at the beginning like we do. Since they always use goat meat on the bone, gosht or meat curry requires long, slow simmering. Their meat is much leaner than our lamb, but it also contains a lot of connective tissue that needs to be softened through long, low-temperature cooking.

Fish, unless it is to be well cooked to preserve it, is added right at the end.

A curry will often be finished with a final flavouring element. This will be something like a generous sprinkling of garam masala, or a specific spice such as black cardamom or toasted, ground cumin. And often there's a fresh element too, like coriander leaves or sliced green chillies. In the north a final charge of yogurt may be added towards the end, and in the south coconut milk. It's common when finishing a dal to add what they call a tarka, which is ingredients such as curry leaves, garlic, ginger, red chillies, onions and mustard seeds dropped into very hot oil and then spooned, sizzling, over the top.

I haven't used any special equipment for my curries but I think you should buy a coffee grinder for dry spices, which will only cost a few pounds, and a mini food processor for such things as turning garlic and ginger into a paste. In India you can buy powerful food processors with interchangeable flasks that will turn both dry spices and wet ingredients like fresh chillies, garlic and ginger into a fine paste. I brought one home and I love it, but unfortunately they don't have all the safety bits required in Europe to stop turning your fingers into purée too.

You can make any curry in a saucepan. I've called in the recipes for a heavy-based pan – or a karahi. I absolutely swear by this Indian pan. It's a round-bottomed steel or aluminium pan with loop handles. You may well have seen them as a serving dish in Indian restaurants, particularly Balti houses. You can buy them cheaply online in the UK. I brought one back from India and use it every day. Make sure you buy a good thick one so the heat disperses evenly. A wok is not really the pan for Indian cooking because it's too thin; it's best for constant stirring and frying. (For more about specific ingredients and equipment, see the back of the book.)

EATING IN INDIA

A meal in India is not a series of courses like in the West. If you look at a restaurant menu you will see there are a few soups and some desserts, but the emphasis is much more on the main course, which will contain at least three dishes but often more. The satisfying subtlety is in the balance between these, the way one dish complements another. You might, for example, have a meat curry, a dal, two vegetable curries, maybe even two types of breads, poppadoms and naans perhaps, two chutneys too, say a fresh green one made with mint and coriander, and a tomato or chilli and ginger relish. There will often be a salad, perhaps sliced cucumber with lime and salt, and normally a raita, a cooling yogurt with mint. I have included a lot of recipes that could be served as first courses, things like the prawn fritters from Calcutta on page 40, or pakoras, momos or kebabs, but these are most often snacks on the street.

As far as sweets are concerned, in an everyday Indian meal you're more likely just to get a fruit drink and finally a sweet masala chai (see page 297 for my take on this). The recipes in the sweet section of the book would be for special occasions or as something to be had mid-morning or mid-afternoon.

In the north, bread is essential to every main meal, and in the south, simple boiled rice, but in any substantial meal there will always be flavoured rice dishes like biryani or a pulao too.

One of the conventions of eating in India, which most Westerners find almost impossible, is eating with their fingers. I must say, I tried often enough while filming, but getting over that feeling of having food all over your right hand is hard to come to terms with. But friends who have mastered the technique say, like all Indians, that Indian food tastes different when eaten with your fingers. This leads me to an observation, which I was thinking about when being filmed eating with my right hand. I was sitting firmly on my left to avoid offending everybody by using it for eating. It is intended for far less savoury purposes. Indians are hygienic in the way they eat and prepare food. It's a developing country so it's vital to be fastidious.

They will always wash their hands before sitting down to a meal and afterwards too. They don't like shaking hands but will greet you by putting their hands together and bowing in an almost prayer-like gesture. This is to express harmony – that their black and white, their yin and yang are in balance – but it's also to avoid passing germs from hand to hand. I noticed as well that, when cooking, they'll never taste food with their fingers. It's all sensible behaviour to keep transferral of germs to a minimum. It's also true to say that you never see a dirty street food stall, and in a country where washing facilities are often rudimentary, people are clean and immaculately dressed, whether it be a suit, a sari or just a shirt and a lungi, the simple cotton loincloth worn by labourers and fishermen everywhere. Their sense of dignity is remarkable. They are often far better turned out than many people in countries where they are lucky enough to have a much better standard of living.

MY PERFECT CURRY

Something must have gone a little wrong with our research team on the coast of Coromandel: they gave us lots of places to visit in Chennai, and some great stories in the former French colonial capital of India, Pondicherry, three hours' drive to the south, but they described the coast between as dirty and featureless. We were just looking for somewhere for lunch when we arrived on the beach of a place with a hard-to-pronounce name, Mamallapuram. Here were four or five fish restaurants right on the sand, and brightly coloured fishing boats with sharp prows all the way along and the Bay of Bengal throwing up some quite considerable surf that day. There seemed to be almost a procession of sacred cows ambling along the beach and a number of beautiful girls dressed in dark reds and blues selling bracelets and necklaces. We were surprised that there were French tourists on this isolated beach in the middle of nowhere. We went into one of the restaurants, called Seashore Garden, and asked if they'd got any good fish. Kingfisher beers arrived at the table, then seafood. They produced a 4-kilo kingfish, three rock lobsters and a large white snapper which would certainly feed us all; they also brought out a colander of very large prawns and half a dozen crabs. 'We'll have the lobsters, prawns and snapper,' I said. 'How will you cook the fish?' They said they'd do it with a tomato masala with tamarind, and invited us into the kitchen.

When a dish as good as this one comes along I become slightly unhinged with excitement. This curry was fragrant with coriander and cloves and sour with the tomato and tamarind and fiery with red chilli, but above all the fish was perfectly cooked at the last minute.

As it happened, my search was over. This curry – here on page 162 – was my favourite curry anywhere in India. My excitement was emphasized by the sheer unexpectedness of finding such food in a place about which we knew nothing, but I suppose, as fish is still my first love, it was inevitable.

DHABA

...are street snacks the most irresistible food in India?

I'm by no means the first person to have come to love the street food of India. From the lamb and spice momos of McLeodganj (page 20) through to koftas, curries and kebabs everywhere, the kerbside stalls and the little hole-in-the-wall places with a couple of tables are amazing sources of culinary excellence. I'm thinking of dhoklas in Gujarat – a savoury soda bread made with rice and chickpea flour and flavoured with turmeric and green chillies (page 24) – and, in the same state, the sweet and tangy potato shreds with cashew nuts, raisins and lentils fried till crisp, then slightly softened with lime juice called, lilo chevda (page 36). Everywhere you go there is steam or fire and tempting smells demanding that you buy.

Calcutta is perhaps the city most famous in all India for its street food. In some ways it's quite a hard city to love. It's visibly falling down around you, so much so that we weren't allowed to point our cameras at some of the buildings sprouting trees. But it's also a city that is almost one big restaurant. When I was there I met Angus Denoon who hails from my part of the UK – Totnes, of 'alternative therapy, make your own yogurt, keep your own goats' fame, in Devon. He took me to ten street vendors of samosas, kebabs, pakoras, fritters and puchkas – the latter named onomatopoeically for the squelching noise the wafer-thin, crisp pastry, shaped to contain a wet filling, makes as you bite into it. The filling is chickpeas, mashed potatoes, masala and lots of black salt which, to someone straight off the plane, was distinctly off-putting as it's heavily imbued with a bad-egg taste of sulphur. Now, however, when I try a fingertip taste of it I am filled with a sense of nostalgia for a city I feel I didn't do justice to, jetlagged as I was. And by the way, salted peanuts with black salt on a bar top have a magnetic quality, especially with a cold Kingfisher beer.

Although Calcutta really brought home to me the skill and remarkable inventiveness of the master chefs of the streets, equally good street food can be found in all the major cities because they are places that attract people from all over the subcontinent, bringing their food with them. I may change my mind next week, next month, next year, but currently my best street food in the world is the pau bhaji of Mumbai (page 42) – soft mashed vegetable curry flavoured with amchur (dried mango powder) and served up with freshly baked soft buns and lashings of soft butter.

I do think that Westerners are absurdly scared of eating anything from a stall. I can understand why – there is a lot of dirt and lack of hygiene around – but the street chefs keep their preparation and cooking areas immaculate and you are possibly safer eating from them than in a restaurant with a hidden kitchen.

I imagine, though, that nobody would hesitate to order some of the wonderful breads that are made outside – naans, pakoras, romali rotis, parathas, poppadoms, idlis, appams and dosas. Everywhere in India there is always someone cooking some bread on the street. In this chapter there are parathas stuffed with the white radish mooli, green chillies, coriander and chat masala (page 23), and the millet flatbreads made with fenugreek leaves and coriander (page 18).

MILLET AND FENUGREEK FLATBREADS
Bajra thepla

Millet sounds rather worthy but I enjoyed eating bajras in Mumbai, and when I tested them back in the UK, I found I couldn't stop eating them. They're very tasty, particularly if you can get fresh methi (fenugreek leaves). I grew fenugreek at one stage in Cornwall, outdoors, without any problem. It's a member of the bean family. You might want to consider sowing a few seeds from a spice jar. If you can't get fresh fenugreek leaves, try pea shoots. They won't have quite the same bitterness but they make an interesting substitute. Flatbreads are perfect for mopping up curry.

MAKES ABOUT 10

RECIPE NOTE
You can find millet flour in a health food shop. Indeed, you can make these with all millet flour for a gluten-free version, though the dough is a little tricky to work with.

2 tbsp natural or
   Greek-style yogurt
½ tsp lemon juice
15g/3 cloves garlic,
   roughly chopped
15g/3cm ginger,
   roughly chopped
1 fresh green chilli, roughly
   chopped, with seeds
200g millet flour (bajra)
50g plain flour, plus extra
   for dusting

Small handful of chopped
   coriander leaves
2 tbsp finely grated jaggery
   or soft brown sugar
2 tsp white sesame seeds
½ tsp salt
50g fresh fenugreek leaves
About 60–80ml cold water
3 tbsp vegetable oil or melted
   ghee, for cooking
Chutneys and relishes,
   to serve (pages 303–5)

Mix the yogurt with the lemon juice and set aside. Put the garlic, ginger and green chilli into a mini food processor with 1 tablespoon of water and blend to a paste.

Put the millet and flour in a bowl and mix in the garlic, ginger and chilli paste, chopped coriander, jaggery, sesame seeds and salt. Stir in the fenugreek leaves, yogurt with lemon juice, and enough of the cold water to form a soft but not sticky dough. Cover and leave to rest for 30 minutes.

Lightly flour a work surface. Take a small piece of dough about the size of a golf ball (weighing about 45g) and roll into a ball then flatten into a disc with your fingertips. As it's a delicate dough, pinch the edges with your fingers to prevent it cracking too much. Dust with a little flour and roll into a disc of about 13cm.

Heat a sturdy frying pan or griddle over a medium heat. When it's hot, add the disc of dough, brushing the top with a little oil or melted ghee. After about 1 minute, flip the dough over and brush the other side with oil or ghee. Turn once or twice more, for a total of about 3 minutes, until golden and lightly charred in places. Keep the bread on a warm plate covered by a tea towel while you make the rest.

TIBETAN STEAMED DUMPLINGS
Momos

This recipe comes from a restaurant in McLeodganj (named after a British divisional commissioner) in Himachal Pradesh, just up the road from the Dalai Lama's residence, and we went there after we'd been to see him. We found him a complete delight. The first thing he said when he met us was, 'You are quite the oldest TV crew I've filmed with.' I suppose I haven't got a leg to stand on but I felt a bit sorry for some of the crew who are only in their forties. These momos were one of the occasions when I couldn't get enough, they were that good. Basically they're just minced lamb, ginger and onion made into a dumpling and steamed, and of course it comes with a fiery Tibetan chilli sauce. It felt special to be sitting down with a crowd of monks, eating our momos and drinking sweet tea.

MAKES 16

For the dough
250g plain flour,
   plus extra for dusting
1 tsp baking powder
¼ tsp salt
150ml warm water

For the filling
175g minced lamb
1 small onion, finely chopped
15g/3cm ginger, finely grated
¼ tsp salt

To serve
Tibetan chilli sauce (page 303)

For the dough, sift the flour, baking powder and salt into a bowl and add enough of the warm water to make a firm but not sticky dough. Knead on a lightly floured surface for 1–2 minutes until smooth, then place in a bowl, cover with a plate and leave to rest for 10 minutes.

For the filling, mix all the ingredients together in a bowl.

To assemble the momos, roll the dough into a long sausage on a lightly floured surface, then cut into 16 pieces. Roll a piece of dough into a ball, then use your fingers to flatten it into a thin disc, about 7cm in diameter.

Put a heaped teaspoon of the filling in the middle of the disc and fold the dough over to make a semi-circle, crimping the edges to seal. Then bring the ends of the semi-circle together and pinch to seal. Alternatively, place the mixture in the middle of the dough, bring the edges up and scrunch together like a purse. Repeat with the remaining dough and filling.

Steam the momos in a lightly oiled steamer for about 15 minutes, until cooked through and piping hot in the middle. Serve hot with the Tibetan chilli sauce.

TIBETAN STEAMED BREAD
Tingmo

These are spongy, slightly gelatinous, little steamed Tibetan buns, pleasingly savoury with garlic, ginger, coriander and tomato. Rather irritatingly moreish on their own, they are addictive when dunked into a rich curry or the very yummy Tibetan red chilli sauce on page 303.

MAKES ABOUT 25–30 INDIVIDUAL ROLLS

For the dough
350g plain flour
1½ tsp baking powder
1 sachet fast-action (easy-blend) yeast
1 tsp salt
200–250ml warm water

For the filling
25g/5cm ginger, finely grated
25g/5 cloves garlic, crushed
½ tsp salt
2 tbsp chopped coriander
2 spring onions, finely chopped
2 tbsp vegetable oil, plus extra for greasing
2 tbsp tomato purée
Butter, to serve

For the dough, combine the flour with the baking powder, yeast and salt in a large bowl and make a well in the middle. Mix in enough of the warm water to give a firm, smooth, but not sticky dough. Knead for 1-2 minutes in the bowl then cover and set aside for about 45 minutes or until risen and almost doubled in size.

For the filling, mix all the ingredients together apart from the tomato purée. Set aside.

Tip the risen dough on to a lightly floured or oiled surface, divide into 4 pieces and roll one piece into a rough rectangle about 5mm thick. Spread with about 1½ teaspoons of tomato purée, then scatter over a quarter of the filling, leaving about a 1cm clear border around the edges. Roll it up fairly tightly, from the long side, as you would a Swiss roll, then cut into slices 3–4cm thick. Repeat with the rest of the dough and filling.

Lightly oil a steamer. Place the rolls sitting upright in the steamer (so the cut sides face down/up), and steam over simmering water, covered, for 25–30 minutes until firm and puffy. Serve warm with butter.

WHITE RADISH PARATHA
Mooli ka paratha

It goes without saying that Amritsar is a very busy city. I can't imagine any of the many cities in India with populations of greater than a million to be anything but a cacophony of noise, traffic, colour, and odours both delightful and terrible. So it's essential to be able to find a peaceful little hotel to rest in. Mrs Rama Mehra's guesthouse, called Ranjit's Svaasá, is just that. She is also an expert in Punjabi recipes and culture, and this recipe of hers is fabulous.

MAKES 5

For the dough
500g chapati flour,
    plus extra for dusting
1 tsp salt
250–300ml cold water
50g ghee or 50ml vegetable
    oil, for frying

To serve
Thick Greek-style yogurt
    and Indian pickles

For the filling
250g white radish
    (daikon, mooli), peeled
    and coarsely grated
1–2 fresh green chillies,
    chopped, with or without
    seeds according to preference
2 tbsp chopped coriander
½ tsp *Chat masala* (page 303)
½ tsp salt
¼ tsp ajwain seeds (carom)

For the dough, combine the flour with the salt and make a well in the middle. Pour in enough of the cold water to give a firm, smooth, but not sticky dough. Knead for 1–2 minutes in the bowl then cover and set aside while you prepare the filling.

For the filling, wrap the radish in a clean cloth and squeeze out excess liquid. Put in a bowl and mix with the chillies, coriander, chat masala, salt and ajwain seeds.

Divide the dough into 10 portions, roll each one into a ball and cover them with a damp tea towel. Using a lightly floured rolling pin, roll out one ball at a time on a lightly floured surface to a circle about 15cm diameter. Spread about a fifth of the spiced mooli filling over this circle, leaving a 5mm border around the edge, then moisten the edge with water. Roll out another portion of dough in the same way and use to cover the mooli filling, pressing down well around the edges to seal. Set aside and repeat with the remaining dough and filling to make 5 stuffed parathas.

Heat a sturdy griddle or frying pan over a medium heat and, when hot, add a teaspoon of ghee or oil and a paratha to the pan. Cook for 2–3 minutes until golden underneath, then flip over, spread with another teaspoon of ghee or oil and cook for a further 2–3 minutes. Do the same with the rest. Serve hot with yogurt and pickles.

GREEN CHILLI AND TURMERIC DHOKLA WITH PRAWNS, CURRY LEAVES AND MUSTARD SEEDS

I got this recipe from Chirayu Amin, the former chairman of the IPL (cricket's Indian Premier League). He has built an annexe to his house, installing a kitchen in which to cook innovative dishes and inviting friends and his family to come and try them. The innovation in this dhokla is the prawns on the top, which is unusual in Gujarat, this being very much a vegetarian state. I had never eaten a savoury cake bread like dhokla before, made with rice and chickpea flour. It is scrumptious.

SERVES 4-6

250g dhokla flour: you can use 165g rice flour mixed with 85g chickpea (gram/besan) flour
120ml water
120g natural yogurt
½ tsp bicarbonate of soda
1 tbsp vegetable oil, plus extra for oiling
1 fresh green chilli, finely chopped, with seeds
1 tsp sugar
1 tsp salt
½ tsp turmeric
1 tbsp lemon juice

For the spiced prawns
2 tbsp vegetable oil
1 tsp black mustard seeds
6–8 fresh curry leaves
¼ tsp Kashmiri chilli powder
2 fresh green chillies, with seeds, finely sliced
250g peeled raw prawns
2 tsp sesame seeds
2 tbsp grated fresh coconut (optional)
2 tbsp chopped fresh coriander
Green chutney (page 303), to serve

For the dhokla, mix together the flour, water, yogurt and bicarbonate of soda, and set aside for 1 hour. Mix in all the remaining dhokla ingredients. Lightly oil a round cake tin, about 18cm in diameter. Pour the dhokla mixture into the tin and place in a steamer, covered, to cook for 15–20 minutes, or until firm and cooked through (don't worry if condensation has dripped on to the top during cooking, as this will be covered with the prawns). When cooked, remove from the tin and cut into slices or 5cm squares, but leave in a circle.

For the spiced prawns, heat the oil in a heavy-based saucepan or karahi over a medium heat, add the mustard seeds, which will spit and pop, then add the curry leaves, chilli powder and green chillies. Fry for 30 seconds, then add the prawns and fry for 3–4 minutes or until pink and cooked through. Stir in the sesame seeds and fry for a further 30 seconds until golden.

Spoon the hot spiced prawns and their oil over the steamed dhokla, followed by the coconut, if using. Finish with the fresh coriander, and serve with green chutney.

SPICY LENTIL SOUP WITH SQUASH, TOMATO AND GREEN BEANS
Sambar

Sambar is served over rice or with dosas or idlis in Tamil Nadu, and most people eat it every day. I watched this being made over a wood fire at Modern Restaurant in Madurai, and ruminated about wood-fired cooking as I perspired in the 90 per cent humidity and 35 degree heat, unhelped by the furnace next to me. The admirable chef, Mr Vallinayagam, was not bothered by the conditions, so enthusiastic was he about cooking his giant pot of sambar over wood, and explaining why it made such a difference – rather as an Italian will do about a wood-fired pizza oven.

SERVES 4–6

For the vegetables
1.5 litres water
100g tur dal (yellow split pigeon peas), well rinsed
1 small onion, chopped
100g carrots, cut into 2cm chunks
100g pumpkin or butternut squash, peeled and cut into 2cm chunks
100g green beans, cut into 2cm lengths
1 medium tomato, chopped
1½ tsp turmeric
1½ tsp sugar
1½ tsp salt

For the masala
50ml vegetable oil
1 tsp chana dal (Bengal gram or split yellow peas)
1 tsp fenugreek seeds
1 tsp coriander seeds
4 dried Kashmiri chillies with seeds
Handful of fresh curry leaves
1 tsp asafoetida

For the tarka
2 tbsp vegetable oil
1 small onion, finely chopped
1 tsp black mustard seeds
1½ tsp fenugreek seeds

For the vegetables, pour the water into a large, deep pan and bring to the boil. Add the tur dal, onion, carrots, pumpkin, green beans and tomato and lower the heat to medium-low. Simmer uncovered for 30 minutes. Stir in the turmeric, sugar and salt and simmer gently for a further 15 minutes or until the dal is soft.

For the masala, heat the vegetable oil in a frying pan over a medium heat. Once hot, add the rest of the masala ingredients and fry for 30 seconds to 1 minute until fragrant. Tip them into a spice grinder or mini food processor, along with the oil, and blend to a paste. Stir the paste into the pan of vegetables.

For the tarka, heat the oil in a clean frying pan over a medium heat and fry the tarka ingredients for 10 minutes, or until the onion is softened and golden brown. Stir this into the pan with the vegetables, along with any oil, and serve.

VEGETABLE PAKORAS

Sometimes I find myself wondering what people would think if they knew that part of what we do in making food programmes is to spend a couple of hours in a rattling minibus driving up windy mountain roads over a dried-up riverbed and into high country dominated by sharp peaks and distant vistas of the Punjab plain. All this to film in a tiny farm the process of turning sugarcane juice into a crystallized form called jaggery by boiling it for an hour or so in a wide, shallow dish over a fire of hardwood from the local forest. Then, when you've met the family and they're so unbelievably happy, relaxed and hospitable, and insist on cooking us the most divine pakoras over a couple of flaming logs, you realize that in a mad world this might just be worth celebrating.

SERVES 4–6

250g chickpea
 (gram/besan) flour
50g self-raising flour
1½ tsp salt
½ tsp turmeric
½ tsp ground coriander
½ tsp ground cumin
250–300ml water
300g potatoes,
 coarsely grated

300g onions,
 coarsely grated
100g fresh spinach,
 coarsely chopped
1 fresh green chilli,
 finely chopped, with or
 without seeds according
 to preference
Vegetable or sunflower
 oil, for deep-frying

Mix both flours, the salt and spices together in a bowl then slowly whisk in the water until you have a batter the consistency of double cream. Add the potato, onions, spinach and chilli and mix well.

Heat the oil in a deep-fat fryer to 180°C, or two-thirds fill a deep saucepan and heat it until a cumin seed dropped into the oil sizzles vigorously. Carefully drop tablespoons of the mixture into the hot oil and fry for 3–4 minutes, until crisp and golden. Drain on kitchen paper and serve.

MULLIGATAWNY SOUP

This is still on the menu at the Madras Club in Chennai. The soup's origins were as a rasam (page 57), known in Tamil as *molo tunny* or 'pepper water', to which the British added chopped mutton or chicken. In her book *Curry*, Lizzie Collingham writes, 'Mulligatawny soup was one of the earliest dishes to emerge from the new hybrid cuisine which the British developed in India, combining British concepts of how food should be presented (as soups or stews, etc.) and Indian recipes.'

SERVES 4–6

For the spice paste
5 tsp coriander seeds
5 tsp cumin seeds
3 tbsp whole black peppercorns
1½ tsp curry powder
1½ tsp turmeric
30g/6 cloves garlic, peeled
20g/4cm ginger, roughly chopped
Small handful each of fresh
    coriander, curry and mint leaves

For the soup
25g butter
3 Indian bay leaves
6 cloves
10g cinnamon stick,
    broken into 2 pieces
100g onion, chopped
50g tomatoes, chopped

50g carrots, thinly sliced
50g celery, thinly sliced
50g leeks, thinly sliced
1 small chicken thigh,
    skin and bone
    removed, chopped
1 tbsp plain flour
2 tsp turmeric
500ml chicken stock
400ml coconut milk
2 tsp salt

To serve
160–240g *Boiled basmati rice*
    (page 313; allow 40g boiled
    rice per person)
3–4 limes, cut into wedges
Sweet mango chutney (page 305)
    or other sweet chutney

Grind the coriander, cumin and peppercorns into a powder, then blend with the remaining paste ingredients in a mini food processor, adding a little water if needed.

For the soup, melt the butter in a heavy-based saucepan or karahi over a medium heat. Add the bay leaves, cloves and cinnamon and fry for 1 minute until fragrant, then stir in the onions and tomatoes and cook for 5 minutes. Stir in the carrots, celery and leeks and cook for a further 5 minutes. Stir in the spice paste and fry for 2–3 minutes, then add the chicken thigh and fry for 2 minutes to coat in the spices. Stir in the flour and turmeric, pour in the chicken stock, bring to a simmer, cover and cook over a low-medium heat for 20 minutes. Stir in the coconut milk and salt at the end. If you like, pick out the cinnamon stick, bay leaves and cloves before serving.

Spoon about 40g of cooked rice into each bowl and ladle over the soup. Finish with a good squeeze of lime juice and serve with sweet chutney on the side.

SPICY SCRAMBLED EGGS
Ande bhujia

In India this makes a great snack with a stack of parathas (page 306) and a dab of chilli garlic relish (page 304). But, more importantly, it's fabulous for breakfast, and since not many people will have gone for breakfast to an Indian restaurant in the UK, it might come as a very pleasant surprise.

SERVES 2–3

2 tbsp vegetable oil
2 large red onions, diced
2–3 fresh green chillies, chopped, with seeds
½ tsp coarsely ground black pepper
3 tomatoes, diced

6 free-range eggs, lightly beaten with ½ tsp salt
1 tsp toasted ground cumin seeds
2 tbsp chopped fresh coriander
Parathas (page 306), to serve

Heat the oil in a frying pan over a medium heat and fry the onions for 10 minutes until golden brown. Add the chillies and black pepper and fry for 2 minutes. Stir in the tomatoes and cook, uncovered, for 5–10 minutes until the tomatoes have softened and reduced to a jammy consistency.

Lower the heat slightly and add the beaten eggs to the pan. Cook for 2–3 minutes without stirring, then gently lift and turn them in the pan. Continue cooking, folding once or twice more, until almost set, then sprinkle over the cumin and fold through. Finish with the chopped coriander and serve with warm parathas.

SWEET AND TANGY POTATO SHREDS
Lilo chevda

This is a snack beloved by Gujaratis, a sweet and sour shredded spiced potato dish. The shredded potatoes are deep fried until crisp, as are the lentils, cashew nuts and peanuts, but plenty of lime juice is sprinkled on just before you start eating so you get this tantalizing mix of crisp bits and soft bits. There's plenty of chilli in it, sweetness from the raisins and sugar, sharpness from the lime juice, and a good sprinkling of salt too. Perfect balance in street food.

SERVES 8

150g chana dal (Bengal gram or split yellow peas), soaked overnight in cold water
1kg potatoes, such as Maris Piper, peeled, coarsely grated
Vegetable oil, for deep frying
Salt
3 tbsp unsalted cashew nuts or peanuts (skinned)

1 tbsp sesame seeds
1 tbsp fennel seeds
½ tsp turmeric
1½ tbsp caster sugar, plus extra to taste
2 fresh green chillies, finely chopped with seeds
2 tbsp raisins
Juice of 1–2 limes

Drain the chana dal and pat dry with kitchen paper. Spread out on a tray lined with a clean tea towel (or more kitchen paper) and leave on one side.

Soak the prepared potatoes in salted water for 20 minutes. Drain, use your hands to squeeze out any excess moisture, then pat dry with kitchen paper.

Two-thirds fill a large, deep-sided sturdy pan with vegetable oil and place over a medium heat. Test it's hot enough by dropping in a piece of potato; it should sizzle and turn golden in about 20 seconds. (Or use a deep-fat fryer heated to 180°C.) Deep-fry the potatoes in batches until crisp and golden. Remove with a slotted spoon and drain on kitchen paper. Season with half a teaspoon of salt and set aside.

Using the same oil, fry the chana dal in batches for about 3–4 minutes, or until they rise to the surface and turn a shade darker. Drain on kitchen paper, and add to the fried potatoes.

Heat a heavy-based frying pan over a low-medium heat. Add the cashew nuts or peanuts and fry for 3–5 minutes, stirring occasionally, until lightly toasted. Add the sesame seeds and fennel seeds and cook for 2–3 minutes, stirring all the time. Remove from the heat and stir in the turmeric, followed by the sugar, half a teaspoon of salt, the chillies and the raisins, then mix with the potatoes and lentils.

Add plenty of lime juice to give a sweet-sour flavour (you may need to add more sugar and salt at this stage to balance the flavour). Serve at room temperature in small bowls as a snack.

PRAWN FRITTERS WITH CHUTNEY AND KACHUMBER FROM THE ALLEN KITCHEN, KOLKATA

I couldn't work out why these prawn cutlets were so delicious; there seemed to be nothing to them, just a simple batter, a bit of lemon, some onion rings and a bottle of mustard sauce. But the very enthusiastic blogger from Calcutta called Kaniska was keen to point out that this tiny little hole in the wall was one of the most popular foodie spots in the city. They may have put a secret ingredient in the batter, but I expect the success lies in using chickpea flour and frying the battered prawns in pure ghee. I consumed a few plates of them while having a thoroughly enjoyable conversation about the almost infinite possibilities of street food in that city. Later I woke up in the middle of the night in my hotel with my head spinning, thinking the pace of life was so frenetic that I was surely locked into a madhouse, albeit with some of the tastiest food I've ever found. This makes a quite soft batter, not a thick, crisp batter like you'd get with fish and chips.

SERVES 4

12 extra large unpeeled
  raw prawns

For the batter
60g plain flour
60g chickpea flour
¼ tsp salt
1 free-range egg
150–225ml water
70g ghee, for frying

To serve
Lemon wedges,
  Mustard chutney (page 304),
  Rick's tomato chutney (page 305)
  or *Chilli garlic relish* (page 304),
  and *Kachumber salad* (page 305)

To prepare the prawns, pull off the head and peel away the shell, leaving the tail intact. Use a small, sharp knife to run down the back of the prawns and pull out the black intestinal tracts, if visible. Then use the knife to cut almost all the way through the prawns and butterfly them open. Flatten them out a little with the palm of your hand. Pat dry with kitchen towel.

For the batter, mix the flours and salt together, whisk in the egg and enough of the water to give a smooth batter the consistency of single cream.

Heat the ghee in a heavy-based saucepan or karahi over a medium heat. Once hot, dip 2 or 3 prawns in the batter and carefully lower into the ghee. Fry for 2–3 minutes, turning once, until crisp and golden and cooked through. Drain on kitchen paper. Repeat with the remaining prawns. Serve with lemon wedges to squeeze over and chutney and kachumber salad on the side.

PAU BHAJI

There's rather a special blog site in Bombay called *Mumbai Boss.* Its strapline is 'Making Sense of the City' – Indians are not without a sense of humour. The food editor, Purve Mehra, took me to a streetside restaurant called Sardar where she felt they made the best pau bhajis in the city, probably the most famous dish there. The indulgence of eating a cracking pau bhaji is similar to that of a beautifully made hamburger: it's about the combination. It was the bhaji, a finely chopped vegetable curry cooked to a soft mash, the freshly baked buns, which seem to arrive from the bakery every half hour, and above all the slab of butter both slathered on to the bun and laid across the bhaji that made the experience so wonderful.

SERVES 4-6

RECIPE NOTE
If you can't get the pau bhaji spice blend, use 2 tsp *Garam masala* (page 303), ¼ tsp ground fennel, ¼ tsp amchur, ½ tsp turmeric and ¼ tsp ground ginger.

350g potatoes, peeled and cut into large chunks
50g butter, plus 15g extra
1 large onion, chopped
2 tsp cumin seeds
400g ripe tomatoes, chopped
1 x 300g can marrowfat peas, drained
3 tsp pau bhaji masala spice blend
1 tsp Kashmiri chilli powder
1 tsp ground coriander
1½ tsp salt
Handful of fresh coriander

To serve
Fresh bread rolls and butter
Large handful of coriander leaves, chopped
1–2 limes, cut into wedges
1 red onion, thinly sliced

Boil the potatoes in a pan of salted water for 10 minutes or until tender. Drain well, then mash.

Heat the 50g of butter in a large sturdy pan over a medium heat. Add the onion and cumin seeds and fry for 10 minutes until softened and golden. Stir in the mashed potato and fry for 1–2 minutes, then add the tomatoes, mix well and cook for 5 minutes, stirring often.

Add the marrowfat peas, all the spices and salt and cook for a further 5 minutes, stirring and mashing the mixture together. Finish by stirring through the remaining 15g of butter and a handful of coriander.

Serve with generously buttered rolls, more coriander, lime wedges and red onion rings.

KAKORI KEBABS

This was named after the place where it was created, Kakori, just outside Lucknow. Introduced by the Mughals, it was originally made with beef, but then it was adapted for lamb, which has a softer texture and didn't offend Hindu sensibilities. In Lucknow it is cooked over charcoal, but a grill or a griddle pan does a pretty good job.

MAKES 10–12

RECIPE NOTE
You will need 10–12 bamboo skewers, soaked in cold water for 10 minutes, or 10–12 lightly oiled metal skewers.

For the browned onion paste
50ml vegetable oil or 50g ghee
2 medium (400g) onions, sliced
3 tbsp hot water

For the spice mix
12 green cardamom pods
2 black cardamom pods
4 cloves
2 tsp coriander seeds
1 tsp cumin seeds
1 blade of mace, or small
   pinch of ground mace
½ tsp black peppercorns
½ tsp white poppy seeds
¼ of a whole nutmeg or
   ¼ tsp ground nutmeg

For the kebabs
500g lean lamb mince
2 green chillies, finely
   chopped, with seeds
10g/2 cloves garlic,
   finely crushed
15g/3cm ginger,
   finely grated
1 tsp salt
100g chickpea
   (gram/besan) flour
25g ghee or clarified
   butter, for basting

To serve
Red onion rings, lime wedges
   and *Green chutney* (page 303)

For the onion paste, heat the oil or ghee in a heavy-based saucepan or karahi over a medium heat, add the onions and fry for 15 minutes until deep golden brown. Transfer to a mini food processor and blend to a paste with the hot water. Set aside.

For the spice mix, extract the cardamom seeds from the pods, then tip all the spices into a spice grinder and blend to a powder.

For the kebabs, tip the lamb into a large mixing bowl with the green chillies, garlic, ginger and salt. Add the browned onion paste and the spice mix, stir well, cover and transfer to the fridge for 3–4 hours.

Tip the flour into a heavy-based saucepan or karahi and place over a medium heat for 5–6 minutes, stirring occasionally, until it darkens and takes on a nutty aroma. Leave to cool, then beat into the lamb mixture. Using wet hands, take a handful of mixture and shape it around the top two-thirds of each skewer, making a sausage shape. Chill in the fridge for 30 minutes before cooking.

Preheat a barbecue, grill or griddle pan until very hot. Cook the kebabs for 10 minutes, brushing with melted ghee and turning frequently until charred in places and cooked through. Serve hot with onion rings, lime wedges, and green chutney.

LAMB SAMOSAS

If you can't get hold of samosa pastry strips (also called samosa pads), use filo spring roll wrappers, or sheets of filo pastry, which you'll need to cut in half lengthways.

MAKES 15–18

For the filling
3 tbsp vegetable oil
2 medium onions, finely diced
20g/4 cloves garlic,
    finely chopped
25g/5cm ginger, grated
1 tsp salt
½ tsp turmeric
½ tsp Kashmiri chilli powder
2 fresh green chillies,
    finely chopped
500g lean lamb mince
1 tsp *Garam masala* (page 303)
Small handful each of coriander
    and mint leaves, chopped
Juice of ½ lime

For the pastry
1 pack samosa pads, spring
    roll wrappers or filo pastry
    sheets (filo pastry should be
    cut into thirds lengthways,
    about 40cm x 9cm each)
1 free-range egg, lightly beaten
Vegetable oil, for deep-frying

To serve
A fresh-tasting dipping
    sauce such as *Green chutney*
    (page 303) or *Tamarind
    chutney* (page 304)

Heat the oil in a heavy-based saucepan or karahi over a low to medium heat and fry the onions for 10 minutes until softened. Stir in the garlic and ginger and fry for a minute. Add the salt, turmeric, chilli powder and green chillies and fry for 1 more minute. Increase the heat to medium-high, add the mince and garam masala and cook for 10–15 minutes, adding a splash of water if it starts to catch, until the mince has browned and cooked through and any excess liquid has evaporated. Leave to cool then stir in the coriander, mint and enough lime juice to sharpen.

To assemble, take a strip of pastry, keeping the rest covered with a damp cloth to prevent drying out. With the long side facing you, make a cone by folding the bottom left corner up and to the right to meet the top of the pastry and form a triangle. Fold it over on itself to the right once more. The opening to the cone will now be on the top of the pastry sheet. Pick it up and two-thirds fill with the mixture. Brush the edges with egg and press to seal, then fold the remaining pastry up and over into a triangle and seal with more egg. Place on a lightly floured tray, and repeat.

Heat the oil in a deep-fat fryer to 180°C, or fill a deep saucepan half to two-thirds full with oil and heat until a cumin seed dropped into the oil sizzles vigorously. Fry the samosas in batches for 5–7 minutes until golden. Drain on kitchen paper and serve with chutney.

LAMB KOFTAS IN YOGURT WITH CINNAMON AND CHILLI
Keema dhai vada

Driving into Thakur Man Singh's huge ancestral property just outside Jaipur in Rajasthan, I had the feeling I'd been there before. Afterwards, in conversation with him, I realized that they'd used his house as the ex-British Raj Club in the film *The Best Exotic Marigold Hotel*, where the character played by Celia Imrie went hunting for rich men. Thakur is royalty, he is a Rajput; I asked his wife Sandhyo what it was like being married to a Rajput and she said, 'I too am a Rajput, we don't marry out of our caste.' They were lovely, very happily married, and for royalty extremely approachable. These koftas make a very good first course or snack.

SERVES 4–6

For the koftas
300g lamb mince
1 tsp ground ginger
1 tsp *Garam masala* (page 303)
½ tsp Kashmiri chilli powder
10g/2 cloves garlic,
   roughly chopped
Small handful of mint leaves
Small handful of coriander
1 tsp salt
3 tbsp vegetable oil, for frying

For the spiced yogurt
400ml natural yogurt
½ tsp ground cinnamon,
   plus extra for sprinkling
Pinch of Kashmiri chilli
   powder, plus extra
   for sprinkling
Parathas or *Chapatis*
   (page 306), to serve

For the koftas, put all the kofta ingredients apart from the vegetable oil into a food processor and blend to a very smooth paste. Take heaped teaspoons of the kofta mixture and, using wet hands, roll into small balls roughly 5cm in diameter.

Heat the oil in a wide frying pan over a medium-high heat and fry the koftas in batches for about 7–10 minutes, turning a few times, until browned and cooked through.

For the spiced yogurt, mix the yogurt in a bowl with the cinnamon and chilli powder, adding a dash of water to thin it down if needed to give it a smooth and runny consistency.

Drizzle the yogurt over the hot koftas, sprinkle with a little more cinnamon and chilli powder, and serve with Indian breads.

KATI ROLLS WITH PICKLED ONION AND GREEN CHILLI SALAD

I ate my first kati rolls at a place called Nizam's in Calcutta. I feel very privileged to have eaten these legendary snacks in arguably the most famous kati restaurant of them all, especially given that kati rolls are now popular on the streets of New York, Sydney and latterly even London. It's a satisfying mix of freshly made paratha with a just cooked layer of omelette rolled up round a kebab flavoured with a cumin and coriander masala plus red onions and green chilli – and it makes you so aware that Indian street food is the best in the world. *Recipe photograph overleaf*

MAKES 6

RECIPE NOTE

You will need 6 bamboo skewers, soaked in cold water for 10 minutes, or 6 metal skewers, lightly oiled, to cook the beef. Once assembled and ready to eat, you can wrap the bottom half of each roll in a strip of greaseproof paper to help hold them together, as they do in Calcutta.

For the beef
500g sirloin or rump steak, cut into 3cm cubes
30g/6 cloves garlic, finely crushed
3 fresh green chillies, finely chopped, with or without seeds according to preference
Juice of 2 limes
1 tsp dried chilli flakes
1 tsp *Garam masala* (page 303)
1 tsp ground coriander
½ tsp salt
2 tbsp vegetable oil
1 tsp *Chat masala* (page 303)

For the pickled onions
2 red onions, peeled, halved and very thinly sliced
2 fresh green chillies, finely chopped, with or without seeds according to preference
3–4 tbsp white wine vinegar or lime juice
1 tsp salt
Handful of coriander leaves, chopped

For the wraps
6 free-range eggs
1 tsp salt
Handful of coriander leaves, chopped
6 *Parathas* or *Chapatis* (page 306), or other flatbreads or small wraps
2–3 tbsp vegetable oil

Heat the oven to its lowest setting, just to keep the parathas warm later on when you assemble the dish. Put the beef in a bowl, add the garlic, green chillies, lime juice, chilli flakes, garam masala, ground coriander and salt and mix together well. Set aside in a cool place to marinate for 1 hour.

For the pickled onions, mix the onions with the chillies, vinegar or lime juice and salt. Set aside while you prepare the rest of the dish.

For the wraps, lightly beat the eggs with the salt and coriander. Heat a frying pan over a medium heat and place a paratha in the pan. Cook for 30 seconds, then drizzle a teaspoon of oil round the edge of the pan so that it runs under the bread. Pour about a sixth of the egg mixture on top of the bread and spread it around. Using a spatula, quickly flip the paratha over so the egg is underneath (most of the egg will fall off the bread into the pan – this is fine). Cook for 1–2 minutes, pressing down on the bread gently with the spatula, until the egg has set. Flip the bread back over and brown the other side for 30 seconds. Repeat with the remaining bread and eggs. Wrap in foil and keep warm in the oven.

Preheat a griddle pan, grill or barbecue to very hot. Drain the beef from its marinade, pat dry with kitchen paper and thread on to the bamboo skewers. Drizzle the kebabs with the vegetable oil and cook for 3–4 minutes, turning every minute or so, until lightly charred in places but still pink in the middle. Remove the meat from the skewers on to a warm plate and sprinkle with chat masala.

To serve, place the warm parathas egg-side-up and arrange the beef down the middle of each.

Drain the onions and chillies from the vinegar or lime juice then toss with the chopped coriander. Generously scatter the onion salad over the meat, then roll up the parathas around the filling and serve.

SABZI

...succulent vegetable dishes, transformed by spice

One of the highlights of my journey through India was finding myself, just after dawn, in a field of cauliflowers outside Deogarh in Rajasthan. We arrived there, from the fort where we were staying in town, in the Rajput's 1920s open-tourer Buick. It must have had at least a six-litre engine and its size and sheer power made it entirely the right vehicle for carrying all, I think, eight of us down narrow country lanes with ruts and potholes. It made modern off-roaders look like Matchbox toys. I was reminded of frosty fields of cauliflowers bordering the Camel Estuary back in Padstow, the difference being that this field was fringed with palm trees, and there were methi (fresh fenugreek) and chillies growing there too.

We watched ladies in yellow, blue and pink saris cutting the cauliflowers and loading them into sacks, then we drove back to the town and enjoyed the early morning market, where a bag weighing 50kg went for 80 rupees, or about £1. Later that day, we lunched on the most perfect curry of potatoes, cauliflower, tomatoes and onions sprinkled with fresh coriander and served with hot chapatis: aloo gobi (see page 90 for my version).

There are over six hundred million vegetarians in India. It's worth pointing out here that in India 'veg' and 'pure veg' above the door of a restaurant means 'with eggs, onions and garlic' for the former and without these for the latter.

With the amazing enthusiasm that everyone has for food, you quickly realize you could spend the rest of your life never eating meat and be happy. The fact is that many Hindus have an aversion to eating meat, and indeed the top caste of Hindus, the Brahmins, are most often vegetarians and rather set the style for everyone else; in other words, it's classy not to eat meat. I think it's one of the main reasons that a journey to India is so fascinating – it challenges you to question whether we really do need to eat so much meat in the West, and when you consider the sort of vegetarian fare that is available it only reinforces that. I mean dishes like dals, made of dried beans or peas and usually mildly spiced and often flavoured with fenugreek, curry leaves, coriander or amchur (dried mango powder) – rich and succulent with ghee and yogurt in the north, while in the south they make them sour with tamarind and tomato, or slightly sweet with coconut.

And then there are the myriad curries made with green vegetables, maybe okra tossed with garlic, onions, garam masala and chilli (page 67) or spinach or other leafy green vegetables wilted with a spicy masala and the mild Indian cheese paneer (the greatest quality of which is that it doesn't break up in cooking).

There is no doubt in my mind, though, that for most Westerners the favourite is an egg curry, which is why there are two in this chapter – one made with green chillies, coconut and turmeric (page 104), the other a deep fiery red Keralan curry called egg roast (page 116).

TIBETAN NOODLE SOUP
Thukpa

When I first tasted thukpa in the front room of Lhamo's tiny apartment in McLeodganj, I was very excited by how such an incredibly straightforward dish of bok choi and noodles with a little flavouring from garlic, ginger and tomatoes could taste so special. Maybe it was having just been to see the Dalai Lama, or the spectacular Himalayan scenery or the friendliness of the largely Tibetan population of that mountain village, home of the Tibetan government in exile, because when I got back to Cornwall and tasted it again it seemed rather bland. I suppose it's a bit like the bottle of rosé you taste in Provence, which is so ordinary back in the UK. Just to be on the safe side, therefore, I've added soy sauce, and accompanied it with the fabulous Tibetan chilli sauce that I also picked up in McLeodganj. Now, even here, it tastes almost as good as I remember it.

SERVES 2-4

4 tbsp vegetable oil
1 medium onion, sliced
1 medium tomato, sliced
1 carrot, sliced
15g/3 cloves garlic,
   finely crushed
15g/3cm ginger, finely grated

1 litre boiling water
½ tsp salt
Baby bok choi
100g dried egg noodles
Soy sauce, to season
Tibetan chilli sauce
  (page 303), to finish

Heat the oil in a heavy-based saucepan or karahi over a high heat. Add the onion, tomato, carrot, garlic and ginger and fry for 4–5 minutes until the vegetables are just starting to soften and take on a little colour. Pour in the boiling water and the salt and bring back to the boil, then add the bok choi and egg noodles and cook for 4 minutes or until the noodles are soft. Season with soy sauce, ladle into bowls and top with a spoonful of Tibetan chilli sauce to stir through.

PEPPER AND TOMATO SOUR SOUP
Thakkali rasam

Like sambar (page 26), rasam is eaten almost every day by southern Indians and is the basis of the Raj dish mulligatawny soup (page 31). It's lightly spiced with pepper and slightly sour with tomato and tamarind. *Recipe photograph overleaf*

SERVES 4–6

1 tbsp ghee
1 tsp black mustard seeds
1 tsp cumin seeds
1 dried Kashmiri chilli, broken into pieces
1 tsp ground black pepper
½ tsp asafoetida
Small handful of fresh curry leaves
4 large tomatoes, chopped
3 green chillies, sliced diagonally

15g/3cm ginger, finely grated
3 tbsp red split lentils
50ml *Tamarind liquid* (page 313)
½ tsp turmeric
1 tsp salt
500ml water
Handful of coriander leaves, chopped, to garnish

Heat the ghee in a sturdy pan or karahi over a medium heat, add the mustard seeds, cumin seeds and red chilli, and fry until the mustard seeds start to pop.

Stir in the black pepper and asafoetida and fry for 30 seconds, then add the curry leaves, tomatoes, green chillies, ginger, red lentils, tamarind, turmeric, salt and water and simmer for 20–25 minutes or until the lentils are tender.

Garnish with chopped coriander leaves and serve.

MY BREAKFAST BHAJI

After a few months of travelling through India I got back to Cornwall and remembered all those early mornings scooping bhajis and aloo dums out of simmering buffet pots, and then going to the counter and asking for a fried egg, which would always come too late as two fried eggs. This was my breakfast every day, but never quite as good as I thought it could be. So the morning after I arrived back in Padstow from Heathrow, I cooked this in the thick karahi I'd lugged back from Kerala, putting everything in it I wanted, knowing that freshly cooked it would have to taste better. And indeed it did.

SERVES 4-6

250g potatoes, peeled
  and cut into 1.5cm cubes
250g carrots, cut into
  2cm x 1cm batons
50ml vegetable oil
2 tsp black mustard seeds
1 medium red onion,
  finely chopped
1 tsp Kashmiri chilli powder

½ tsp turmeric
2 tomatoes, chopped
½ tsp salt
1 tsp *Garam masala* (page 303)
50ml water

To serve
4–6 free-range eggs, fried
Indian breads (pages 306)

Cook the potatoes in boiling salted water for about 10 minutes until tender. Remove with a slotted spoon, set aside, then cook the carrots in the same water for about 3 minutes until just tender but still with a bit of crunch.

Heat the oil in a heavy-based saucepan or karahi and fry the mustard seeds until they start to pop, then add the onion and fry over a moderate heat for 5 minutes until softened. Add the chilli powder and turmeric and fry for 30 seconds, then add the potatoes, carrots, tomatoes, salt, garam masala and water, and cook for 3–5 minutes, stirring to break up the potatoes a bit, until the tomatoes are reduced and jammy.

Serve with Indian breads and a fried egg.

SMOKY AUBERGINE WITH TOMATO, GINGER AND FRESH CORIANDER
Bainghan ka bharta

I must say I'd never heard of kitty parties before I went to Ambica Aggarwal's house in Hoshiarpur in the Punjab, which is next to the flour mill run by her husband Rishi's family. Kitty parties are part of Indian life for ladies of all levels of society. Each group pays so much a week into a kitty – it can be as little as £2 and as much as £50 – and they take it in turns to host a party that will include lunch. Standing talking to Ambica and her charming friends, it reminded me most of a book club back in the UK, i.e. men are not particularly welcome. It is, in fact, a very sensible way of socializing for young married mums, particularly in the rural areas. The big money gets spent in Delhi, where it's more a matter of style. Ambica says children insist on this dish.

SERVES 4–6
AS A SIDE DISH

2 large aubergines
2 tbsp mustard oil
(see page 312)
250g onions, peeled and sliced
25g/5cm ginger, finely grated
350g fresh tomatoes, chopped

½ tsp salt
½ tsp Kashmiri chilli powder
½ tsp *Garam masala* (page 303)
Handful of fresh coriander,
roughly chopped, to garnish

For an authentic flavour, use tongs or a skewer to hold the aubergines directly over a gas flame until the skin becomes charred and blackened. Alternatively, place them under a very hot grill, turning a few times, to get a similar but less smoky result. Leave to cool slightly then peel off the skin. Roughly mash the flesh in a bowl and set aside.

Heat the mustard oil in a heavy-based saucepan or karahi over a medium-high heat until smoking, add the onions and fry for 10 minutes, then add the ginger and fry for a further 2 minutes. Stir in the tomatoes, salt and chilli powder, and cook for 5 minutes until reduced slightly. Add the aubergine flesh, heat through, and stir in the garam masala. Serve garnished with coriander.

SEASONAL VEGETABLE CURRY
Kair sangri

By no means all the recipes in this book require a lot of preparation and mixtures of spices. In as much as Indians ever produce anything like our accompanying vegetables, this dish would be it. You fry some spices, onions, garlic and chilli in ghee, then chuck in whatever vegetables you like and fry for a few minutes before adding some roughly chopped tomatoes and simmering everything together until cooked. That's it, job done.

SERVES 4–6

30g ghee or 2 tbsp vegetable oil
1½ tsp cumin seeds
4 cloves
2 medium onions, thinly sliced
15g/3 cloves garlic, chopped
2 green chillies, sliced into rounds
1 tsp salt

300g small cabbage, such as hispi or spring pointed, shredded
180g cauliflower, cut into small florets
250g tomatoes, chopped
75g peas, fresh or frozen and defrosted

To serve
Boiled basmati rice (page 313) or *Chapatis* (page 306)

Heat the ghee in a heavy-based saucepan or karahi set over a medium-high heat, add the cumin seeds and cloves and fry for 30 seconds until aromatic. Add the onions and fry for 10 minutes or until softened and lightly golden. Stir in the garlic, chillies and salt, and fry for another 30 seconds.

Add the cabbage and cauliflower and fry for 3–4 minutes, then stir in the tomatoes and simmer uncovered for 8 minutes until the vegetables are just tender, adding a splash of water if it looks too dry. Add the peas and cook for a further 2 minutes. Serve with rice or chapatis.

DRY-FRIED OKRA WITH GARLIC, CUMIN AND GARAM MASALA

Unlike the majority of dishes in India, this must be served as soon as it's cooked.
Recipe photograph overleaf

SERVES 4-6

3 tbsp vegetable oil
1 large onion, sliced
10g/2 cloves garlic, finely chopped
1 tsp ground cumin
1 tsp Kashmiri chilli powder
½ tsp turmeric
450g okra, sliced in half lengthways
1 tsp salt
Juice of ½ lemon
1 tsp *Garam masala* (page 303)

Heat the oil in a sturdy saucepan or karahi over a medium heat. Add the onion and fry for 10 minutes until softened and golden brown, then add the garlic and fry for 2 minutes. Stir in the cumin, chilli powder and turmeric and fry for 5 minutes. Add the okra, salt and lemon juice, cover and cook for 10 minutes. Stir in the garam masala and cook, uncovered, for 5 minutes. Serve.

SPINACH CURRY WITH GREEN CHILLI, YOGURT AND INDIAN CHEESE
Sag paneer

This is a common vegetable dish in northern India. It is designed to be made with any leafy, spinach-like vegetable, of which there are many in the early morning markets in the Punjab. Over here, spinach is the obvious choice (or English spinach, as it is known in Australia), but another good choice would be Swiss chard leaves. In this case, longer cooking of the leaves will be necessary and you will need to add a little water. It's always a good idea to have a jug of water handy when making a curry, whether to stop spices catching and burning or just to make a bit more 'gravy'.

SERVES 4

75g ghee or butter or 75ml vegetable oil
400g onions, finely chopped
30g/6cm ginger, grated
30g/6 cloves garlic, finely chopped
1 tsp turmeric
1 tsp *Garam masala* (page 303)
1 tsp Kashmiri chilli powder
400g paneer, cut into 3cm cubes

1 tsp salt
500g spinach, washed and roughly chopped
1 fresh green chilli, thinly sliced, with seeds
100g natural yogurt
Handful of coriander leaves, chopped
Spoonful of double cream, to finish (optional)

Heat the ghee, butter or oil in a heavy-based pan or karahi and fry the onions, ginger and garlic on a medium heat for 10–12 minutes. Stir in the turmeric, garam masala and chilli powder followed by the paneer, and fry for 2–3 minutes until the cubes are well coated in the spices. Add the salt, spinach, green chilli and yogurt, put a lid on the pan and let the spinach wilt for a couple of minutes. Remove the lid and simmer for 3–4 minutes or until reduced to a thick, creamy sauce. Sprinkle with the chopped coriander and serve. You may like to finish with a spoonful of double cream for a richer dish.

DRY CURRY OF CABBAGE, CARROT AND COCONUT
Thoran

Thoran is a dry vegetable curry from Kerala made from whatever fresh vegetables are around – snake beans, unripe jack fruit, sag (leafy vegetables), even green tomatoes. Taking a very common and normally in season vegetable in the UK, like cabbage, I've worked on this dish to produce my own version, which means I've kept faithful to the essential ingredients of mustard seeds, green chillies, ginger and, above all, grated coconut, but I have made the dish as quick as possible to produce.

SERVES 4–6

3 tbsp coconut oil
   or vegetable oil
2 tsp black mustard seeds
2 tbsp fresh curry leaves
1 tsp cumin seeds
2 dried Kashmiri chillies,
   each broken into 3 or 4 pieces
30g/6cm ginger, finely grated
   into a paste
½ tsp turmeric
1 tsp salt
½ tsp coarsely ground
   black pepper

250g hispi or pointed spring
   cabbage (or spring greens),
   shredded into 5mm pieces
2 carrots, diced
2 fresh green chillies, sliced
   into thin rounds, with seeds
100g fresh or frozen coconut
   flesh, blitzed in a food
   processor or grated

To serve
Boiled basmati rice (page 313)
   and poppadoms

Heat the oil in a heavy-based saucepan or karahi set over a medium heat, and when hot, add the mustard seeds followed by the curry leaves, cumin seeds and dried chillies. Stir for about 30 seconds, then add the ginger paste, turmeric, salt and black pepper and fry for 30 seconds.

Stir in the cabbage and carrots and cook, covered, over a medium heat for 5–7 minutes or until the vegetables are tender, adding a splash of water if they start to stick to the pan.

Stir in the green chillies and coconut, heat through for a minute and serve. Serve with rice and poppadoms.

QUICK-FRIED BEANS, CARROTS AND PEAS WITH FRESHLY GRATED COCONUT
Poriyal

A simple but lively vegetable dish, cooked quickly with spices and finished with a handful of fresh coconut. 'Poriyal' in Tamil means fried vegetable – this recipe can be made using any variety of vegetables. I tasted this at Modern Restaurant at Madurai, where it was served on a banana leaf with a number of other dishes. I noticed too that a potato and a cabbage version were also served to worshippers at the Meenakshi Temple. I love the Meenakshi Temple; it's absolutely worth travelling to Madurai to visit it. An overwhelming combination of towers with gaily painted bas-relief figures, chambers, high ceilings, a holy pool for immersion and life-size statues everywhere. One I noted was of a half-naked, comely woman whose breasts had been polished by hundreds of thousands of hands. *Recipe photograph overleaf*

SERVES 6

2 tbsp vegetable oil
4 dried Kashmiri chillies
Handful of fresh curry leaves
1 tsp black mustard seeds
1 tsp cumin seeds
½ tsp coriander seeds
1 tsp mung dal

For the vegetables
150g peas
150g green beans,
    cut into 1cm pieces
150g carrots, cut into
    1cm cubes
½ tsp salt
75ml water
50g fresh or frozen coconut
    flesh, blitzed in a food
    processor or grated

Heat the vegetable oil in heavy-based saucepan or karahi over a medium heat. Add the chillies, curry leaves, mustard, cumin and coriander seeds, and dal, cover with a lid and fry for 1–2 minutes until fragrant.

Add the peas, beans, carrots and salt and fry for 2 minutes, then pour in the water, cover and cook for 5–7 minutes until the vegetables are just tender. If any water remains, remove the lid and boil rapidly for a minute until it evaporates. Stir in the coconut and serve.

A CREAMY POTATO AND ASPARAGUS CURRY WITH CINNAMON, FENNEL AND BLACK CARDAMOM
Mandra

Visiting Himachal Pradesh finally made me realize that vegetarian dishes are the rule rather than the exception in India. I must say as a serious meat-eater it takes some getting used to, but in India you do get used to it because the amount of spicing makes everything so interesting. This dish, mandra, also made me realize the importance of Ayurveda in Hindu cooking. There's normally no onion or garlic in this dish, because it is served regularly at religious festivals and those ingredients are regarded as 'hot', ones that inflame the passions, but I've sacrilegiously put some in. This mandra was cooked for me by Mrs Bina Butail from a family of tea planters who produce kangra tea, and before she started to cook she gave us all a cup of green leaf tea, slightly sweetened, no milk, one teaspoon of tea leaves per person. It was exquisite; I'd love to see it available in the UK. She was a charming lady, very nervous when cooking in front of the camera, but with the most lovely kitchen. I have to confess I went nosing in her spice cupboard, and she let me try the half a dozen different pickles that a good Indian housewife delights to make. She made the mandra with a type of yam called Gandali. I found it a little dry, but she also makes it with potato and asparagus, as I've done here. I've slightly reduced the amount of oil and yogurt too, as it's a bit much for our taste, though not theirs. This is also good with peas instead of asparagus.

SERVES 4

For the spice blend

6 cloves
5cm piece of cinnamon stick
2 Indian bay leaves
1 large black cardamom
    pod, seeds only
2 tsp Kashmiri chilli powder
1 tsp cumin seeds
1 tsp coriander seeds
1 tsp turmeric
1 tsp salt
1 tsp fennel seeds

For the mandra

800g potatoes (King Edward
    or Maris Piper are good),
    peeled and cut into
    2–3cm chunks
4 tbsp mustard oil (see page 312)
    or vegetable oil
1 large onion, chopped
15g/3 cloves garlic,
    finely chopped
1½–2 tsp sugar
200g asparagus, trimmed
    and cut into 5cm pieces
    at an angle
250ml natural yogurt
60ml double cream
Juice of ½–1 lime

Place all the spices for the blend in a spice grinder (or use a pestle and mortar) and work to a powder.

For the mandra, cook the potatoes in a large pan of boiling salted water for 8–10 minutes, or until tender. Drain thoroughly. Heat the oil in a heavy-based saucepan or karahi over a medium heat and fry the onion for 10–15 minutes until deep golden. Add the garlic and fry for 1 minute. Stir in all the spice blend and 1½ teaspoons of sugar and fry for 30 seconds or until the spices release a warm fragrance.

Increase the heat slightly, add the potatoes and toss around in the spices for 1–2 minutes, then stir in the asparagus and yogurt. Simmer for 5 minutes – adding 2–3 tablespoons of water if it starts to catch – until the asparagus is just cooked. Stir in the cream and enough water to give a smooth consistency, simmer for 2–3 minutes, then add the lime juice. Taste and add a little more sugar, salt or lime juice if needed. Serve.

VEGETABLE MAKHANAWALA

I remember this lovely rich vegetable curry from years ago in Goa on the menu of the Reef restaurant at the Ronil beach resort in Baga. I always love to eat it, and I am just as interested in the pronunciation of makhanawala – I just find it a very pleasing name. I think it means 'with lots of butter and cream'. I've made this with potatoes, carrots, green beans, cauliflower, peas and have kept all the vegetables except the potatoes slightly al dente, a happy contrast to the spicy, buttery tomato sauce.

SERVES 4-6

800g mixed vegetables, such as potatoes, carrots, green beans, cauliflower and peas, chopped into 4–5cm pieces

For the sauce
50g ghee
1 medium onion, sliced
25g/5 cloves garlic, finely crushed
25g/5cm ginger, finely grated
400g tomato passata
1 tsp Kashmiri chilli powder

½ tsp ground coriander
½ tsp ground cumin
½ tsp ground cinnamon
¼ tsp turmeric
½ tsp *Garam masala* (page 303)
1 tsp desiccated coconut
1½ tsp salt
25g cashew nuts
½ tsp caster sugar
75ml natural yogurt
4 tbsp double cream
Handful of chopped coriander leaves, to finish

Cook the potatoes and carrots separately in boiling salted water for 10 minutes or until just tender, then drain.

For the sauce, heat the ghee in a heavy-based saucepan or karahi over a medium heat. Add the onion and fry for 10 minutes until softened and golden, then stir in the garlic and ginger and fry for 1 minute. Stir in the tomato passata and bring to a simmer for 5 minutes. Add all the spices, coconut, salt and 100ml water, and simmer for a further 10 minutes.

In a mini food processor, or using a pestle and mortar, blend the cashew nuts to a paste with 2 tablespoons of water. Stir this into the sauce, followed by all the vegetables, apart from the potatoes, another 100ml water, and simmer for 10 minutes until the vegetables are cooked through. Stir in the potatoes, sugar, yogurt and cream and cook for a further 2–3 minutes. Garnish with coriander and serve.

POTATO AND PEA CURRY WITH TOMATO AND CORIANDER
Aloo dum

Aloo dum is possibly the most common vegetable curry in India. It's almost like chips with everything here, aloo dum with everything there. It's either easy to make or hard, depending on what you want to do with it. If I was describing it to somebody I'd just say boil potatoes, fry them with garam masala, add some tomato, chilli, turmeric and salt and it's done; then, if you like, throw in frozen peas just before the end. It's a dish that will repay a little more attention to detail as well, however. This recipe comes from Calcutta and was cooked by Seema Das's charming, intelligent and optimistic daughter Ishika in their small flat right in the centre of the city. Seema was our guide in Calcutta and I'd like to take this opportunity to thank her for her conscientiousness while looking after us and her infectious love of the city she lives in. The only slight drawback with Ishika's cooking was that Seema was, as all Indian mothers do, breathing down her neck, so it took quite a long time to film because Ishika kept deferring to her. *Recipe photograph overleaf*

SERVES 6-8

For the fried potatoes
1kg potatoes, peeled and
  cut into 3cm chunks
4 tbsp mustard oil
  (see page 312)
  or vegetable oil
1 tsp turmeric

For the sauce
3 tbsp vegetable oil
2 Indian bay leaves
¼ tsp asafoetida
1 medium onion,
  very finely chopped
30g/6 cloves garlic,
  finely crushed
25g/5cm ginger, finely grated

1 tsp Kashmiri chilli powder
1 tsp ground cumin
1 tsp ground coriander
½ tsp amchur (dried
  mango powder)
½ tsp turmeric
½ tsp salt
200g tomato passata
2 green chillies, sliced
  lengthways into thin strips,
  with or without seeds
  according to preference
100ml water
150g frozen peas
1 tsp *Garam masala* (page 303)
Handful of chopped coriander
  leaves, to finish

Boil the potatoes in salted water for 8 minutes until just tender, then drain well. Heat the oil in a heavy-based saucepan or karahi over a medium-high heat, add the potatoes and fry for 5 minutes until golden, then add the turmeric and fry for 30 seconds. Remove from the heat.

For the sauce, heat the oil in another pan over a medium-high heat. Add the bay leaves and fry for 1 minute, then add the asafoetida and stir. Add the onion and fry for 5 minutes, then add the garlic and ginger and fry for 5 minutes until softened and lightly golden. Add the chilli powder, cumin, coriander, amchur, turmeric and salt and fry for 1 minute, then add the tomato passata, green chillies and water and stir together. Add the fried potatoes, reduce the heat to medium, cover the pan and cook for 10 minutes, adding a splash of water if anything catches on the bottom of the pan.

Add the peas and garam masala and cook uncovered for 3–4 minutes, until the peas are cooked. Garnish with fresh coriander and serve.

POTATO AND CAULIFLOWER CURRY
Aloo gobi

Like aloo dum (page 86), this is just another everyday vegetable curry which I always make a beeline for in India. I'm particularly fond of aloo gobi with a fried egg on top for breakfast. It's also good with raita and chapatis.

SERVES 4

3 tbsp sunflower oil
1 medium onion,
    roughly chopped
20g/4 cloves garlic,
    finely chopped
1 tbsp *Garam masala* (page 303)
2 tsp Kashmiri chilli powder
1 tsp salt
2 medium tomatoes, chopped
500g potatoes, peeled and
    cut into 3cm chunks

400ml water
1 medium cauliflower,
    cut into rough 5cm florets
Handful of chopped
    coriander leaves, to finish

To serve
Raita (page 304) and
    Chapatis (page 306)

Heat the oil in a heavy-based saucepan or karahi over a medium-high heat, add the onions and fry for 7 minutes until golden. Add the garlic and fry for 1–2 minutes, then stir in the garam masala, chilli powder and salt, and fry for 1 minute. Add the tomatoes and cook for 2 minutes until slightly softened, then add the potatoes and pour in the water. Bring to a simmer, cover and cook over a medium heat for 10 minutes. Add the cauliflower and cook, covered, for 7–8 minutes, or until the cauliflower and potatoes are tender.

Scatter with fresh coriander and serve with raita and chapatis.

VEGETABLE AND COCONUT STEW
Avial

I picked up this Keralan vegetable stew of beans, carrots, sweet potatoes and cucumber at a house owned by photographer and flautist Ashok Koshy, where I was filmed cooking twenty-five recipes. His cook Mallika's recipes are dotted throughout the book. On the last day of filming we had a party. I cooked my favourite fish curry, the Madras curry on page 162. Mallika produced, amongst other things, a delicious vegetable thoran (page 72) and this avial. Ashok invited some of his chums over, including a retired Bollywood star called Babu Antony who had played Tarzan, his cousin who sang excellent American country and western songs, and two architects, one of whom bemoaned the lack of proper planning regulations in India. There were also an Indian couple from Houston with a very smiley, podgy baby, whom my wife Sarah couldn't leave alone, Ashok's utterly beautiful sister called Kanchana, and his 91-year-old mother, who was in very good form, complaining to Sarah, who got on very well with her, that people didn't drive fast enough these days. A memorable afternoon, and a lovely vegetable dish. *Recipe photograph overleaf*

SERVES 4-6

For the vegetables
750g mixed vegetables,
   cut into 5cm x 1cm batons –
   runner beans or drumstick
   beans, carrots, green beans,
   sweet potato (peeled),
   cucumber (peeled and
   seeds removed)

For the paste
200g fresh or frozen coconut
   flesh, roughly chopped
1 small onion, roughly chopped

For the seasoning
1 tbsp coconut oil
3 fresh green chillies,
   chopped, with seeds
½ tsp turmeric
½ tsp Kashmiri chilli powder
2 tbsp *Tamarind liquid*
   (page 313)
1 tsp salt

To finish
Small handful of curry leaves
1 tbsp coconut oil, warmed

Cook all the vegetables apart from the cucumber in boiling salted water until tender. Drain and return to the pan.

Blend the coconut and onion in a mini food processor to a coarse paste. Stir into the hot vegetables, along with all the seasoning ingredients. Cover with a lid and cook over a low heat for 10 minutes so the vegetables steam gently, adding the cucumber for the last minute just to heat through.

To finish, stir in the curry leaves and drizzle with coconut oil.

BUTTERNUT SQUASH IN SWEET TAMARIND MASALA

Think of this as an accompaniment to a couple of other curries, more like a chutney than anything else, even though you might find yourself scoffing large quantities of it as it is so sweet and sticky and pleasingly hot. The sourness of the tamarind balances the dates, raisins and jaggery. It's very quick to cook. I like to serve it with a lamb rogan josh (page 258) or a jungli maas (page 260) and a dal or two.

SERVES 4

4 tbsp mustard oil (see page 312) or vegetable oil
½ tsp fenugreek seeds
1 tsp nigella seeds
50g ginger, finely grated
1 small butternut squash or pumpkin, peeled, seeds removed, flesh cut into 1cm cubes (about 400g prepared weight)
2 fresh green chillies, finely chopped, with seeds

½ tsp Kashmiri chilli powder
1 tsp ground coriander
75g dates, finely chopped
2 tbsp desiccated coconut
2 tbsp raisins
2 tsp jaggery or soft brown sugar
1 tsp salt
2–3 tsp *Tamarind liquid* (page 313)
Handful of chopped fresh coriander, to finish

Heat the oil in a heavy-based saucepan or karahi over a medium heat, add the fenugreek seeds and fry for about 30 seconds, then add the nigella seeds and ginger and cook for a minute.

Stir in the squash, green chillies, chilli powder and ground coriander, cover and cook on a low-medium heat for about 10 minutes.

Add the dates, coconut, raisins, jaggery and salt to the pan, stir well, replace the lid and cook for a further 10 minutes, stirring occasionally, until the squash is tender but still holding its shape.

Stir in the tamarind and taste, adding a little more tamarind if needed – it should be sweet and tangy. Scatter over the coriander and serve.

CHICKPEA CURRY
Chana masala

I would hazard a guess that chana masala or chickpea curry is the most popular vegetarian curry in India. I sternly instructed my son Jack, who tested this recipe for me, only to use proper dried chickpeas soaked and boiled. He stole down to the deli, grabbed a jar of Spanish garbanzos and used the liquid with the chickpeas in place of some of the cooking water. It was a triumph. Maybe I'm too strict on tins and jars.

SERVES 4-6

250g dried chickpeas, soaked in cold water overnight, or 625g (drained weight) of tinned or jarred chickpeas
1 tbsp vegetable oil
1 large onion, finely chopped
25g/5 cloves garlic, finely crushed
25g/5cm ginger, finely grated
2 fresh green chillies, finely chopped, with seeds

2 tsp ground coriander
2 tsp ground cumin
2 tsp Kashmiri chilli powder
½ tsp ground turmeric
300g vine-ripened tomatoes, chopped
2 tsp salt
1 tsp *Garam masala* (page 303)
1 tbsp lemon juice
Handful of coriander leaves, chopped

If using dried, soaked chickpeas then first drain them. Bring a large pan of water (without salt) to the boil, add the chickpeas and simmer over a medium heat for 45 minutes to an hour, or until soft but still holding their shape. Drain, reserving some of the cooking liquid to add to the sauce if needed. If using chickpeas from a can or jar, omit this stage.

Heat the oil in a sturdy pan or karahi over a medium heat. Add the onions, and fry for 10–15 minutes until softened and golden brown. Stir in the garlic, ginger and green chillies and fry for 1 minute, then add the ground coriander, cumin, chilli powder and turmeric and fry for 30 seconds. Add the tomatoes, chickpeas, salt and 300ml water or chickpea cooking water and bring to a simmer. Cook for 20 minutes, stir in the garam masala and lemon juice, scatter with the coriander and serve.

KIDNEY BEAN CURRY
Rajma

One of the surprising things I discovered on my journey through India and staying, I have to confess, in nice hotels, was that the cooking in such places was actually very good, even the buffets, where you are presented with, say, twenty curries, the majority of them vegetarian. Rajma would be included in the buffet of every one of those hotels in the north of India, and with dishes like these I would have no problem being a vegetarian. As I've said in the recipe, it's a good idea to mash some of the beans against the side of the pan just before serving, to thicken what the Indians always call the gravy a little.

SERVES 6-8

350g dried red kidney
   beans, soaked overnight
   with cold water to cover
1 tsp turmeric
50ml vegetable oil
3 medium onions, chopped
20g/4 cloves garlic,
   finely chopped
75g ginger, finely chopped
   or grated

1 tsp salt
1 tsp Kashmiri chilli powder
1 tsp *Garam masala* (page 303)
125ml thick Greek-style yogurt

To serve
Boiled basmati rice (page 313)
   and lime wedges

Drain the soaked beans, put them in a heavy casserole pot, cover with fresh water and sprinkle in the turmeric. Place over a medium heat, bring to a simmer, then lower the heat and simmer uncovered for 1–1½ hours, or until the beans are tender, topping up with water if the pot starts to look dry.

Heat the oil in a large pan or karahi over a medium heat and fry the onions, garlic and ginger for 10 minutes or until tinged golden brown. Add the salt, chilli powder and garam masala and fry for 30 seconds, then stir in the yogurt and cook for 5 minutes.

Add the drained cooked beans to the onion mixture, along with enough of the cooking liquid to just cover the beans (topping up with water if necessary) and simmer for 10 minutes, mashing a few beans against the side of the pan with the back of a spoon to thicken the gravy. Serve with basmati rice and wedges of lime.

VEGETARIAN CURRY WITH INDIAN CHEESE, TOMATOES AND PEPPERS
Paneer jalfrezi

According to a poll featured in the British Curry Club's in-house magazine, the jalfrezi is now the most popular choice in Britain's Indian restaurants. In many Indian restaurants, however, they list 'jalfrezi', 'rogan josh', 'dopiaza', and then simply change the main ingredient from mutton to chicken to vegetable, so you get the impression it's always the same sauce. This jalfrezi is specifically for paneer, the Indian cheese, and is little more than a stir-fry, which is perfect for the main ingredient. Paneer is easier and easier to get now, and available in most larger supermarkets. I have on occasion used the Cypriot cheese halloumi, which is similar though saltier. *Recipe photograph overleaf*

SERVES 2–4

3 tbsp vegetable oil
1½ tsp cumin seeds
1 dried Kashmiri chilli, whole with seeds
25g/5cm ginger, finely shredded
3 small onions, thinly sliced
1 fresh green chilli, chopped, with or without seeds
1 red or yellow pepper, seeds removed, cut lengthways into 5mm-thick strips
1 green pepper, seeds removed, cut lengthways into 5mm-thick strips

1 tsp salt
½ tsp turmeric
1½ tsp Kashmiri chilli powder
250g paneer, cut into 3cm x 1.5cm pieces
3 tomatoes, cut into strips
1 tsp wine vinegar
½ tsp toasted ground cumin seeds
¾ tsp *Garam masala* (page 303)

Heat the oil in a heavy-based saucepan or karahi over a medium heat and add the cumin seeds, whole dried red chilli and about two-thirds of the shredded ginger, and fry for 30 seconds until aromatic.

Add the onions and green chilli and fry for 5–6 minutes until the onions are just softening but not browned and still have a little crunch. Add the peppers, salt, turmeric and chilli powder, and fry for a further 3–4 minutes.

Lower the heat, add the paneer to the pan and gently stir everything together for about 5 minutes, then add the tomato and heat through. Stir in the vinegar, ground cumin and garam masala, scatter with the remaining shredded ginger, and serve.

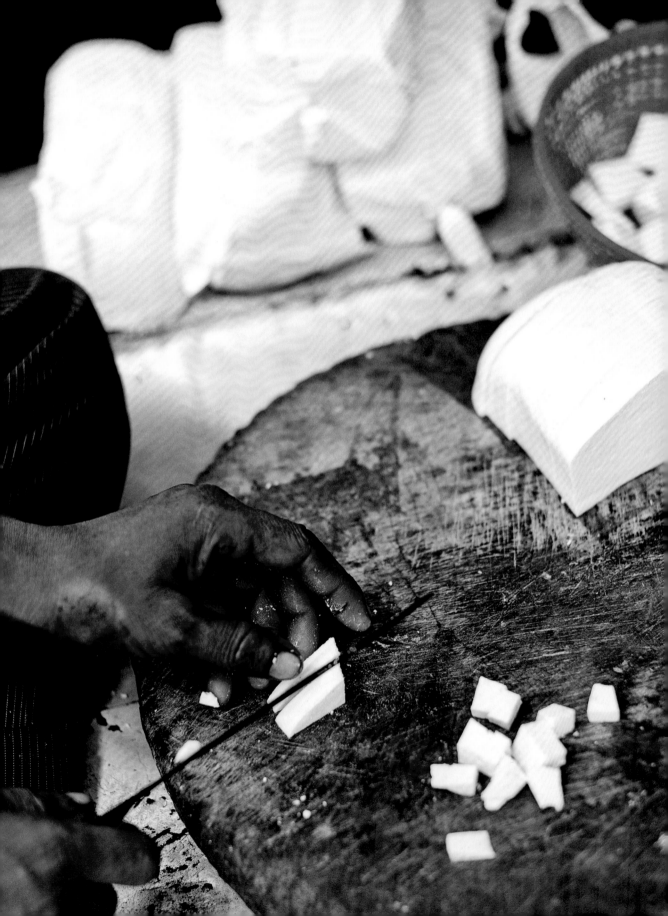

WHOLE EGGS IN COCONUT MASALA
Egg molee

Writing this before the TV series that accompanies the book comes out, I'm not sure whether the recipe we filmed in the home for destitute women in Calcutta will appear in the programme because the cook was so bad-tempered. A shame if it doesn't, because it's a nice, simple coconut masala with whole eggs, which are quickly fried before being finished off in the curry. I particularly remember the day there because I was so overwhelmed by the women's stories.

SERVES 4

3 tbsp mustard oil (see page 312) or vegetable oil
6 hard-boiled free-range eggs, peeled and left whole
1 tsp turmeric
1 tsp Kashmiri chilli powder
400ml coconut milk
2 medium red onions, very thinly sliced
20g/4cm ginger, finely shredded

3 fresh green chillies, thinly sliced, with seeds
½ tsp salt
1 tsp sugar
Handful of coriander leaves, chopped
½ tsp *Garam masala* (page 303)

To serve
Boiled basmati rice (page 313)

Heat the oil in a heavy-based saucepan or karahi over a medium heat, add the whole eggs and fry for 1–2 minutes until lightly coloured, then add the turmeric and chilli powder and cook for another 30 seconds. Stir in the coconut milk and bring to a simmer.

Add the onions, ginger, chillies and salt, and simmer for 5 minutes, until the coconut milk has reduced in volume by half and the onions are just softened, adding a splash of water if it becomes too thick. Stir in the sugar and coriander and sprinkle with garam masala. Halve the eggs, and serve with rice.

YELLOW DAL WITH TOMATO, TURMERIC AND FRIED KASHMIRI CHILLIES
Tarka dal

This is the dal I make most often, mainly because it's so incredibly easy and quick, but also because finishing it off with a tarka is so special. A tarka is a last-minute fry of spices and chilli which you pour, still sizzling, on top of the dal in the dish.

SERVES 4-6

For the dal
200g yellow tur dal or
 chana dal, soaked in cold
 water for 1 hour, drained
2 medium tomatoes, chopped
1 medium onion, chopped
4 green chillies, slit
 lengthways, with seeds
10g/2 cloves garlic, peeled,
 left whole
Small handful of fresh
 curry leaves
1 tsp salt
½ tsp turmeric

For the tarka
2 tbsp vegetable oil
1 tsp black mustard seeds
2 shallots, finely chopped
4 dried Kashmiri chillies,
 each broken into 3 pieces
About 15 fresh curry leaves
Handful of coriander leaves,
 roughly chopped, to garnish

Put the dal into a large saucepan and cover with water by about 4cm. Add all the remaining dal ingredients, bring to the boil, then lower the heat to medium and simmer for 45 minutes to an hour for tur dal, up to an hour and a half for chana dal, until the dal is soft but still with a little bite. Use a potato masher to break up about half of the lentils, being sure to leave plenty of texture.

For the tarka, heat the oil in a pan over a medium heat, add the mustard seeds and fry for 30 seconds until they pop, then stir in the shallots, Kashmiri chillies and curry leaves and fry for 2–3 minutes until the shallots are softened and golden.

Spoon the tarka on top of the dal, sprinkle with fresh coriander leaves and serve.

BLACK DAL
Maa ki dal

After a few weeks in India, I began to find a meal without dal unthinkable, and black dal is the one that always finds itself on your plate. It has a viscosity you become very attached to, and for me it was the first vegetarian dish that made me realize I could live without meat. It's not just the flavour of the dal, but also the interesting mix of spices and the essential finish of shredded ginger and chopped coriander with a lick of ghee – though I'm perfectly happy to use butter at home instead.

SERVES 6-8

350g whole urid (small black bean/sabut urid)
2 tsp Kashmiri chilli powder
50ml mustard oil (see page 312) or vegetable oil
3 Indian bay leaves (optional)
6cm piece of cinnamon stick
1 medium red onion, chopped
300g tomatoes, roughly chopped
1½ tsp toasted ground cumin seeds
1½ tsp turmeric
1½ tsp ground coriander

1½ tsp *Garam masala* (page 303)
¼ tsp asafoetida (optional)
2 tsp salt

To finish
25g butter or ghee
20g/4cm ginger, finely shredded
Handful of fresh coriander, roughly chopped

To serve
Indian breads (pages 306) or *Boiled basmati rice* (page 313)

Wash the beans in plenty of cold water, then cover with fresh water by 4cm and leave to soak overnight. The next day, put the beans and their soaking water into a large pan with the chilli powder and 2 teaspoons of the mustard oil. Bring to a simmer, cover the pan with a lid and cook over a low heat for 1½–2 hours, topping up with a little water when needed, until the lentils are completely tender.

Meanwhile, heat the remaining oil in a frying pan over a medium heat, add the bay leaves, if using, and cinnamon stick and fry for 1 minute until fragrant, then add the onion and fry for 10 minutes until golden. Stir in the tomatoes, spices and salt and simmer for 10 minutes until reduced slightly.

Add the tomato mixture to the cooked lentils and simmer for 15 minutes. Stir in the butter, finish with the shredded ginger and chopped coriander and serve with Indian breads or rice.

SULTAN'S PIGEON PEA DAL
Tur dal sultani

This was cooked for me by Pankaj Bhadouria at her cookery school in Lucknow, which she has opened on the back of becoming the first Indian MasterChef winner in 2010. It's a notably sour-tasting dal because of the large amount of yogurt in it, one of those tastes in Indian cuisine which you start off finding a bit overpowering and end up seeking out. Pankaj finished cooking the dal by putting a betel leaf on top of it, then a hot piece of charcoal, pouring ghee over the charcoal and putting a lid on. The flavour of smoky butter imbued the dal marvellously. However, I've left this out here, but by all means have a go if you're happy with red-hot charcoal and a lot of butter smoke in your house.

SERVES 4-6

250g tur dal (yellow split pigeon peas), soaked for 15 minutes, drained
1.5 litres water
1½ tsp salt
1 tsp Kashmiri chilli powder
250ml milk
250g natural yogurt
125g double cream
Pinch of saffron threads soaked in warm water for 15 minutes
10 cardamom pods, seeds only, finely ground
6 cloves, finely ground

For the tarka
1 tbsp ghee
40g/8 cloves garlic, thinly sliced
1 tbsp cumin seeds

To finish
2 green chillies, finely chopped
Handful of mint leaves, finely chopped
Lemon wedges

Boil the dal in the water with the salt and chilli powder for 30 minutes or until completely tender. Drain well, then mash with a potato masher to a smooth consistency. Add the milk, yogurt, cream, saffron and its soaking water, cardamom and cloves. Bring to a simmer and cook over a low-medium heat, covered, for 5 minutes.

For the tarka, heat the ghee in a small pan over a medium heat. When hot, add the garlic and the cumin seeds and fry for 2 minutes until the garlic is just turning golden. Pour it over the dal and swirl through gently. Scatter with the chopped green chillies and mint, and serve with lemon wedges to squeeze over.

TAMARIND RICE
Puliyodharai

This was being prepared in the kitchen of the Meenakshi Temple in Madurai. There, once the rice is cooked, it is pressed against a stone surface by hand; they believe this gives it additional flavour. I remember remarking at the time that religion in India seems to be very much part of everyday life. At the temple they have a kitchen that cooks food free for worshippers, but they also have another kitchen where they cook food to be sold and taken away, which is blessed by a priest. It would be rather like if you went to York Minster and came away with a Yorkshire pudding blessed by the archbishop. This is a very nice rice dish, a bit nutty from the mustard seeds and dal, with just the right amount of sourness from the tamarind and heat from dried red Kashmiri chillies.

SERVES 4

175g basmati rice
100ml *Tamarind liquid*
  (page 313)
100ml water
6 dried Kashmiri chillies,
  sliced in half lengthways
1 tsp cumin seeds

50ml vegetable oil
Handful of fresh
  curry leaves
1 tsp black mustard seeds
1 tbsp mung dal (skinned
  and split mung beans)
1 tsp salt

Put the rice in a saucepan and cover with 300ml water. Bring to a simmer over a high heat then stir once, turn the heat to low, cover the pan and cook for 7–8 minutes or until all the water is absorbed and the rice just tender. Stir gently with a fork to separate the grains.

Put the tamarind liquid into a wide pan with the extra water, the chillies and cumin seeds. Bring to the boil over a medium-high heat and bubble for 2–3 minutes or until reduced to the consistency of double cream.

Heat the oil in a large frying pan over a medium heat. Add the curry leaves, black mustard seeds and mung dal and fry for 1 minute until fragrant, then stir in the tamarind mixture. Cook together for 2–3 minutes, by which time the mung dal should be soft enough to eat but still with some bite, then add the rice and mix everything together. Cook for 2–3 minutes until the rice is piping hot, then serve.

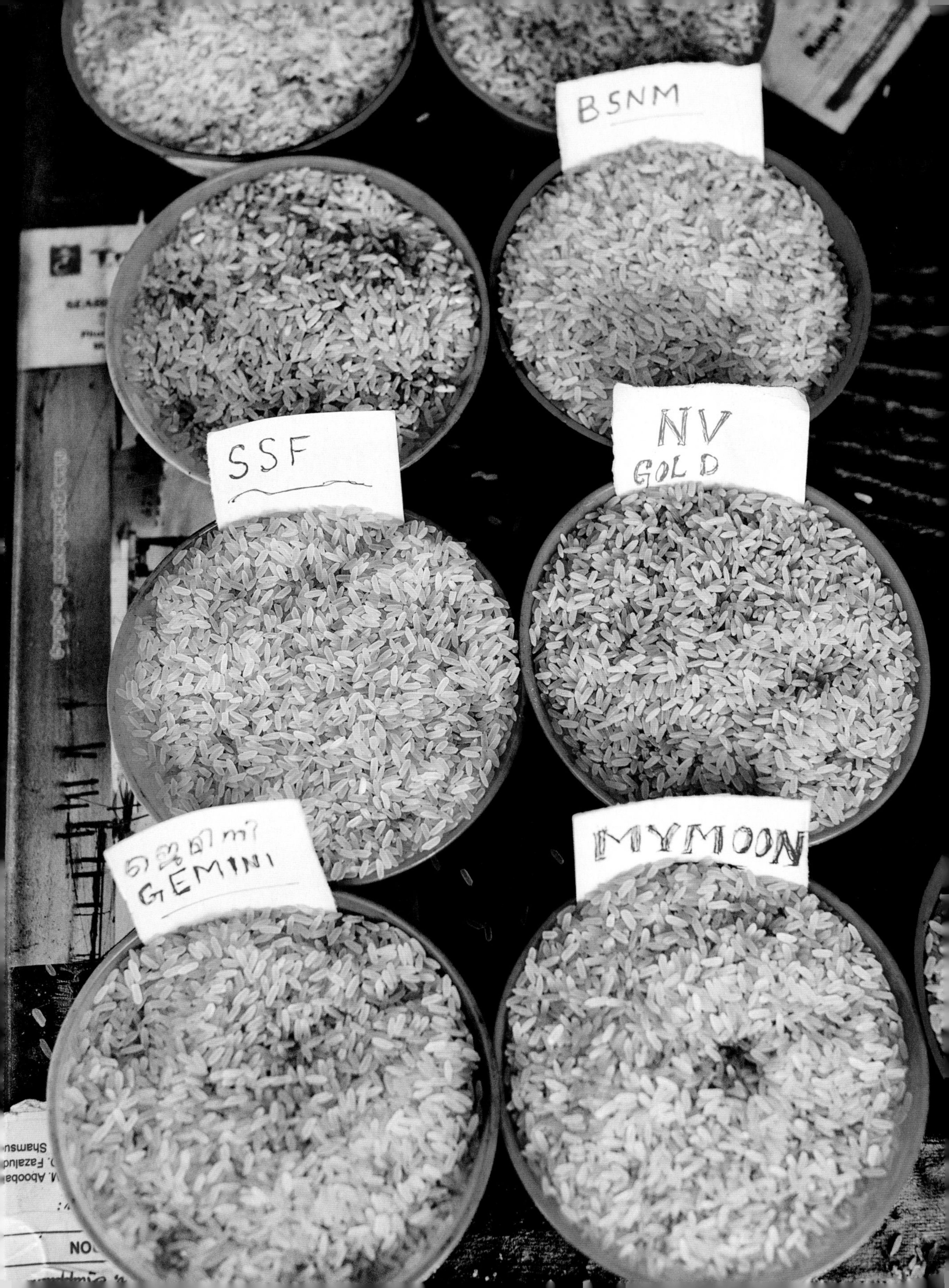
BSNM
SSF
NV
GOLD
GEMINI
MYMOON

EGG ROAST EN ROUTE TO THEKKADY

I find that a good recipe can often be found at the lunch place a driver selects for Western sensibilities – i.e. air conditioning and toilets that don't smell too bad. It never ceases to amaze me how good the cooking in these restaurants can be, though the places themselves are completely devoid of atmosphere, with the curtains drawn against the glare of a hot day, lots of tiled surfaces, maybe a picture on the wall of Ganesha the elephant god, lord of success and destroyer of evils, riding on a mouse. I was intrigued to see 'egg roast' on the menu of the Green Mango multi-cuisine restaurant in the hotel ABM Grand in Theni, between Madurai and Thekkady. It's a popular dish in Kerala. Nobody quite knows why it's called an egg roast because they are actually boiled, peeled, then simmered in a pan with an intense red masala flavoured with Kashmiri chillies, tomato and coconut oil. I love an egg curry and this is possibly my favourite.

SERVES 4-6

6 free-range eggs
2 tbsp coconut oil
Small handful of fresh
   curry leaves
1 tsp fennel seeds
250g onions, sliced
2 dried Kashmiri chillies,
   torn into pieces
20g/4cm ginger,
   finely chopped
20g/4 cloves garlic,
   finely crushed

1 tsp ground coriander
1 tsp ground cumin
1 tsp Kashmiri chilli powder
1 tsp ground black pepper
½ tsp turmeric
400g tomato passata
1 tsp salt

To serve
Handful of fresh coriander
   leaves, chopped
Chapatis (page 306)

Bring a pan of water to the boil, add the eggs and cook for 10 minutes. Drain and run under cold water before peeling.

Heat the coconut oil in a heavy-based pan or karahi over a medium heat. Add the curry leaves and fennel seeds and fry for 30 seconds, then add the onion and fry for 10 minutes until softened and golden brown. Add the dried chillies, ginger and garlic and fry for 2–3 minutes, then stir in the ground coriander, cumin, chilli powder, black pepper and turmeric, and fry for 30 seconds. Add the tomato passata and salt and simmer for about 10 minutes until rich and reduced, then add the whole eggs, put a lid on and simmer for 4–5 minutes to heat the eggs through. Sprinkle with the chopped coriander and serve with chapatis.

MOREL PULAO

The foothills of the Himalayas must be inundated with lovely wild mushrooms, and I've always wondered how the people there cook them. Having made this a few times, it's obvious to me now that a pulao is a perfect vehicle for them, being delicately flavoured and allowing the mushrooms to take centre stage. It's rather similar to a mushroom risotto. I have to confess I used dried morels for this, not fresh, but I like the rather smoky flavour they have. This would work well with any mushrooms – chanterelles, girolles, ceps and even common or garden button mushrooms. *Recipe photograph overleaf*

SERVES 4-6

3 tbsp vegetable oil
½ tsp cumin seeds
6 green cardamom pods, bruised
5cm piece of cinnamon stick,
    broken in half
1 medium onion, finely chopped
20g/4cm ginger, finely grated
15g/3 cloves garlic,
    finely crushed
50g dried morels, covered
    in boiling water and soaked
    for 30 minutes, drained

1½ tsp salt
350g basmati rice,
    soaked in cold water
    for 30 minutes,
    drained and rinsed
500ml cold water

To finish
Handful of fresh
    coriander, chopped
2–3 green chillies,
    chopped, with seeds

Heat the vegetable oil in a heavy-based saucepan or karahi over a medium heat, add the cumin seeds, cardamom pods and cinnamon, and fry for 30 seconds. Add the onion and fry for 10 minutes until softened and golden.

Stir in the ginger and garlic and fry for 2 minutes, then add the drained morels and salt. Increase the heat slightly, add the rice, and fry for 1 minute to coat in the oil.

Pour in the cold water and bring to the boil, then reduce the heat to low-medium and cover with a lid. Cook for about 8–10 minutes, or until all the water has been absorbed by the rice. Turn off the heat and leave to stand with the lid on for 10 minutes.

Scatter with fresh coriander and green chillies, and serve.

MACCHI

*...the incomparable taste of fish and shellfish,
coconut, tomato, tamarind and spice*

After we'd been filming in India for about six weeks, David, the director, started getting withdrawal symptoms. Everywhere we'd been so far was inland and he, and very soon I, began to pine for the sea. Actually, quite a few of the dishes we'd eaten or watched being cooked up to that point had been for what the Indian call sweet water fish, which are river fish such as the Bengali fish hilsa (shad) and rui (a type of carp). Indeed one of my favourite fish dishes in the book, Amritsari fish (see page 164), came from that busy city Amritsar, home of the Golden Temple and stuffed full of handsome Sikhs.

But since there are about four and a half thousand miles of coastline around India, and my first love is seafood, we guiltily abandoned inland Gujarat in favour of Mumbai, the Coromandel coast of Tamil Nadu and, lastly and most deliciously, the sandy beaches and brackish Backwaters of Kerala. There is something about filming along the coast that seems right – whether it's out on the high seas, or on a beach somewhere watching the frantic energy as the early morning boats are pulled up and the catch unloaded and auctioned there and then so that it can be iced and off to market before the day gets too hot, or mooching around the fishermen's harbour in Chennai or the Sassoon Dock in Mumbai, getting in the way of the bustling activity and being told in no uncertain terms to move.

Above all, though, the flavour of fish curry in India is for me the most memorable of all dishes the country has to offer. I may have said this once or twice before but the Indians see nothing amiss in marrying delicate fish with chilli, coriander, turmeric, cinnamon and plenty of salt. Most fish curries are quickly cooked, usually with some souring element such as tamarind, tomato, green mango or the ultra-sour, dark smoky flavour of kokum. Further north it's more likely to be cooked with a big sting of mustard such as the mustardy fish curry on page 178.

European cooks would hold up their hands in horror at this decimation of delicacy – about red chilli and clove masala with lobster they would say 'Dreadful!', but the Indians couldn't care less and, frankly, if the seafood is absolutely fresh, nor could I. The natural sweetness works in some mysterious way with extreme spice, and if we were more accustomed in this country to a fish curry made with fresh kingfish, pomfret, mahi mahi or snapper, we'd all be fanatical about fish.

There are more recipes in this chapter than any other. It contains the perfect curry for me, the snapper with tamarind and tomato from Mamallapuram (also known as Madras fish curry, page 162), but close runners-up would be the mild, creamy coconut-based prawn molee (page 138) or the Chettinad crab curry (page 151), which is incredibly spicy. I have to say that all the fish curries of southern India are a little on the hot side and I may have become slightly immune to the heat, so I've been very careful in these recipes to keep them true to the flavours I remember without going too far.

DRY PRAWN CURRY WITH KOKUM
Prawn peera

Peera is a dry vegetable or prawn curry from Kerala – the sauce is really reduced and thick so it just coats the prawns. The souring agent in this is kokum, a dried fruit of the mangosteen family, which they tend to use more than tamarind. I must say I'm a complete fan of kokum and tend to use it quite often, even when the recipe calls for tamarind, because it has a delicious fruity flavour as well as sourness. Use tamarind if you can't get kokum.

SERVES 4

4 pieces kokum
(or 150ml *Tamarind liquid*, see page 313)
50g ginger, finely chopped
4 green chillies, with seeds, halved lengthways and each half chopped into thirds
2 dried Kashmiri chillies, torn into pieces
4 shallots, thinly sliced

Small handful of fresh curry leaves
¼ tsp turmeric
½ tsp salt
125g fresh or frozen coconut flesh, blitzed in a food processor or grated
2 tbsp coconut oil
400g large peeled raw prawns

If using kokum, wash it, place in a bowl, cover with 150ml boiling water and leave to soak for 30 minutes. Drain, reserving the soaking water.

Put the ginger, green chillies, dried red chillies, sliced shallots, curry leaves, turmeric and salt into a pan with the kokum pieces and 100ml of the reserved kokum soaking water (or all of the tamarind liquid), the grated coconut and coconut oil. Mix well and bring to a simmer over a medium heat. Simmer for 5 minutes, adding a splash of water if it starts to stick, then add the prawns and simmer for a further 3–4 minutes, until the prawns are cooked and the sauce reduced to a thick consistency. Serve.

COCONUT PRAWN CURRY
Chingri malai

This recipe is from Kewpies, Rakhi Dasgupta's famous restaurant in Calcutta, and is one of her signature dishes (along with the mustardy fish on page 178). This book is about my search for the perfect curry, and this one went straight into the top ten.

SERVES 4

4 medium onions, peeled, 2 finely sliced, 2 roughly chopped
25g ghee
2 Indian bay leaves or 3cm piece of cinnamon
½ tsp *Garam masala* (page 303)
15g/3cm ginger, finely grated
15g/3 cloves garlic, finely crushed

1 tbsp turmeric
1 tsp Kashmiri chilli powder
250g large peeled raw prawns
280ml coconut milk
1 tsp salt
1 tsp sugar
150ml water
Boiled basmati rice (page 313), to serve

Blend the 2 roughly chopped onions in a mini food processor to a fine paste, adding a splash of water if needed.

Heat the ghee in a heavy-based saucepan or karahi over a medium heat, add the bay leaves or cinnamon stick and fry for a minute until fragrant. Add the sliced onions and fry for 10 minutes until golden, then stir in the garam masala and fry for 30 seconds. Add the onion paste, ginger, garlic, turmeric and chilli and fry for 5 minutes, stirring often, or until the onion paste is golden, adding a splash of water if it catches on the bottom of the pan.

Stir in the prawns, cook for 1 minute, then pour in the coconut milk, salt, sugar and water. Bring to a simmer and cook for 5 minutes or until the sauce has reduced by half and the prawns are pink and cooked through. Serve with rice.

PRAWNS WITH FRESHLY GRATED COCONUT, GREEN CHILLIES AND MUSTARD SEEDS
Chingri daab

There are quite a few recipes for prawn and coconut in this book, but I love the combination. This is different in that I'm using coconut flesh as well as the milk. It's a popular dish in Bengal, where of course both prawns and coconut abound. It's normally served in a whole green coconut there, but that's a bridge too far for us. I would suggest serving it, as in Bengal, as a little course in its own right, but it's also delicious with some rice and flatbreads.

SERVES 4–6

2 tbsp black mustard seeds
4–6 tbsp mustard oil (see page 312)
   or vegetable oil
1 medium onion, thinly sliced
1 tsp turmeric
250ml coconut milk
250g fresh or frozen coconut
   flesh, blitzed in a food
   processor or grated

1 tsp salt
350g peeled raw prawns
4 fresh green chillies,
   with seeds, cut lengthways
   into sixths
Handful of chopped
   coriander, to finish

Put the mustard seeds into a mini food processor and add 2 tablespoons of water. Blend for a minute then add another 2 tablespoons water and continue blending until the seeds start to break up (this can take a minute or two of persistent blending; add more water if you're having trouble). Keep blending until you have a rough paste that resembles wholegrain mustard, adding a splash more water if needed. Set aside.

Heat the mustard or vegetable oil in a heavy-based saucepan or karahi over a low-medium heat. Add the onion and fry for 10 minutes. Add the blended mustard paste, turmeric, coconut milk, grated coconut and salt. Bring to a boil then simmer for 4–5 minutes. Add the prawns and green chillies and simmer for a further 3–4 minutes until the prawns are pink and cooked through. Scatter with coriander and serve.

SAUTÉED PRAWNS AND COURGETTES WITH SALTED LEMON, CORIANDER AND BASIL

This recipe comes from the Hotel de l'Orient in Pondicherry. In the French quarter they cook a fusion of Indian and French dishes, which they call Creole cooking. This is a simple dish of prawns with garlic and olive oil but also contains pickled lemon, curry leaves, chilli and garam masala. This was the recipe the chef Ashok cooked for me in the courtyard of the beautiful eighteenth-century French villa, now a hotel. The leaves thrown in at the end could be different, but if you can get the curry leaves that really sets the seal on the Creole element. *Recipe photograph overleaf*

SERVES 2–4

50ml olive oil
5 banana shallots, thinly sliced
20g/4 cloves garlic, finely chopped
20g/4cm ginger, finely shredded
250g large peeled raw prawns
1 medium courgette (about 150g), thinly sliced
30g pickled lemon, thinly sliced
½ tsp finely chopped thyme leaves

½ tsp finely chopped rosemary leaves
½ tsp Kashmiri chilli powder
½ tsp *Garam masala* (page 303)
½ tsp ground black pepper
1 tsp salt
Small handful each of fresh coriander, curry and basil leaves

Heat the olive oil in a heavy-based saucepan or karahi over a medium heat. Add the shallots, garlic and ginger and fry for 5 minutes until softened. Increase the heat to medium-high and stir in the prawns, courgette and pickled lemon. Fry for 1–2 minutes, then add the thyme, rosemary, chilli powder, garam masala, black pepper and salt and fry for a further 2–3 minutes, stirring often, or until the prawns are pink and cooked through.

Stir through the coriander, curry and basil leaves and serve.

PRAWN CURRY WITH GREEN CHILLIES FROM CALCUTTA

If you refer to my recipe for egg curry from Calcutta on page 104, you'll notice in the introduction that it came from a home for destitute women, and before the cook did actually lose her temper – because she was so busy and we were in her way with our camera and lights – she cooked this curry for the restaurant attached to the home, which is open to the public. It took about ten minutes to make and seemed to me as good a recipe for curried prawns as you could get.

SERVES 4

1 small onion,
    roughly chopped
40g/8 cloves garlic,
    roughly chopped
30g/6cm ginger,
    roughly chopped
30g ghee
1 tbsp Kashmiri
    chilli powder
3 Indian bay leaves
200g natural yogurt
1 tsp ground cinnamon

1 tsp ground cardamom (or the
    seeds from 30 pods, ground)
½ tsp ground cloves
½ tsp turmeric
1 medium tomato, sliced
2 green chillies, sliced, with
    or without seeds according
    to preference
1 tsp salt
½ tsp sugar
500ml water
400g peeled raw prawns

Blend the onion, garlic and ginger together in a mini food processor to a rough paste; alternatively, you can grate them finely. Heat the ghee in a heavy-based pan or karahi over a medium heat, add the onion, garlic and ginger paste, and the chilli powder, and fry for 10 minutes until softened and golden.

Add a splash of water, scrape up any browned bits from the bottom of the pan, then add the bay leaves and mix in the yogurt. Stir in all the spices followed by the tomato, chillies, salt and sugar. Pour in the water, bring to a simmer and simmer for 5 minutes to reduce in volume by about half. Add the prawns and simmer for a further 5 minutes until the prawns are cooked. Serve.

PRAWN MOLEE

All the tourists I met in Kerala who had been to Philipkutty's Farm, on an island in a lake in the Keralan Backwaters, singled it out as having the best food anywhere and, when I finally met Anu Mathew, I understood why. She's a very intelligent and enthusiastic cook who produced, among other things, this remarkable dish. In fact, she made it with karimeen, a local fish, but a few nights later I had almost the same molee with prawns at the Malabar Hotel in Fort Cochin, and as I'd already got oodles of recipes for karimeen, I decided to use Anu's recipe for prawns instead. When I tasted it, I remember thinking this could quite easily be a recipe for a fish and white wine and cream sauce from some very smart French restaurant, so delicate was it.

SERVES 4-6

2 tbsp coconut oil
¼ tsp ground black pepper
3 green cardamoms, lightly
    bruised with a rolling pin
6 cloves
2 medium onions, thinly sliced
15g/3 cloves garlic, thinly sliced
25g/5cm ginger, finely shredded
2 green chillies, slit lengthways,
    seeds removed
1 tsp salt

Small handful of fresh
    curry leaves
Small pinch (⅛ tsp) turmeric
400ml coconut milk
1½ tsp toddy or white
    wine vinegar
500g large tail-on raw prawns
2 tomatoes, thinly sliced into
    rounds, to garnish
Boiled basmati rice
    (page 313), to serve

Heat the coconut oil in a heavy-based saucepan or karahi over a medium heat. Add the pepper, cardamoms and cloves and fry for 1 minute until fragrant. Add the onions and fry for 5 minutes until translucent, then stir in the garlic, ginger, chillies, salt and curry leaves and fry for 1 minute.

Add the turmeric, coconut milk and vinegar. Bring to a simmer and simmer for 4–5 minutes until reduced slightly, then add the prawns and simmer for a further 4 minutes until the prawns are cooked. Scatter the tomatoes on top, turn off the heat, cover the pan and set aside for 3–4 minutes. Serve with rice.

KAVITA'S MADRAS PRAWN CURRY

I was rather looking forward to having a Diwali breakfast with Kavita Chesetty and her husband, but due to the ever-changing nature of filming we had to go on Chennai's Marina Beach and talk about Madras curry powder while walking towards the camera looking like it was the most natural thing in the world – doubly irritating because when we arrived at the house, breakfast of fluffy idlis and fish and chicken curries with soft dosas had long been cleared away. It was a special morning feast because of Diwali, the Hindu festival of lights, which is as important as our Christmas. Kingfisher beers were offered and Kavita rattled through this recipe, which was excellent, and before long we were sitting down to a lunch of prawns and fish curry. I really like this; it's refreshingly simple. Kavita has a food blog called malli.in, and a very successful shop selling cup cakes called Cupcakes Amore; a very modern young Indian mum doing things about town.

SERVES 4

60ml vegetable oil
1 tbsp black mustard seeds
1 medium onion, finely chopped
24 fresh curry leaves
15g/3 cloves garlic,
    finely chopped
2 tsp Kashmiri chilli powder
½ tsp ground coriander
½ tsp turmeric
100g tomato passata
100ml *Tamarind liquid* (page 313)

3 green chillies, each cut
    lengthways into 6 pieces,
    with or without seeds
    according to preference
1 tsp white wine vinegar
½ tsp salt
500g large tail-on raw prawns
Handful of coriander leaves,
    chopped, to finish
Boiled basmati rice
    (page 313), to serve

Heat the oil in a heavy-based saucepan or karahi over a medium heat, add the mustard seeds and fry for a minute until they start to pop. Add the onion and half the curry leaves and cook for 10 minutes until the onion is softened and golden brown. Add the garlic and fry for a further 3 minutes, then stir in the chilli powder, coriander and turmeric and fry for 30 seconds.

Stir in the passata, tamarind liquid, chillies, vinegar and salt, then add the prawns and 2–3 tablespoons of water and simmer for 4–5 minutes until the prawns are cooked. Stir in the remaining curry leaves and chopped coriander and serve with plain rice.

SQUID CURRY

This recipe is taken from Karkera Canteen in Fort Mumbai. Krishna Pujari, my guide in Mumbai, took me to this 'hole in the wall' restaurant, saying it's the best place to eat curry in the city. It's certainly the most atmospheric, if a bit of a squeeze. The limited kitchen preparation tables are turned into customer tables during lunch hour and yet they manage to serve five hundred meals a day. Most of it is seafood, enormously quickly cooked and all the better for it. *Recipe photograph overleaf*

SERVES 4

For the masala paste
1 tsp coriander seeds
1 tsp cumin seeds
1 tsp black mustard seeds
1 tsp fenugreek seeds
25g/5 cloves garlic, peeled
3 fresh red chillies,
  stalks removed
1 tsp turmeric
50g fresh or frozen coconut,
  grated or blitzed in a food
  processor
50ml water

For the squid
3 tbsp vegetable oil
1 tsp black mustard seeds
1 small onion, thinly sliced
25g/5 cloves garlic, finely sliced
20g/4cm ginger, finely shredded
2 fresh green chillies, with seeds,
  thinly sliced at an angle
400g cleaned squid in rings
½ tsp Kashmiri chilli powder
1 small tomato, chopped
1 tsp salt
75ml water
50ml *Tamarind liquid* (page 313)
1 tsp jaggery or ½ tsp soft
  brown sugar
Handful of fresh coriander
  leaves, chopped, to finish

For the masala paste, tip the coriander seeds, cumin seeds, mustard seeds and fenugreek seeds into a spice grinder and grind to a powder (or use a pestle and mortar). Transfer to mini food processor with the garlic, chillies and turmeric, and blend to a paste, then add the coconut and water and blend again.

For the squid, heat the oil in a sturdy pan or karahi over a medium heat, add the mustard seeds and fry for 30 seconds until they begin to pop, then stir in the onion and fry for 5 minutes. Add the garlic, ginger and green chilli and fry for a minute, then stir in the squid, the masala paste, chilli powder, tomato, salt and water and simmer for 2–3 minutes until the squid is cooked but still tender. Stir in the tamarind liquid and jaggery or sugar. Scatter over fresh coriander and serve.

KERALAN SEAFOOD BIRYANI

I've often thought there's a connection in cooking terms between paella and biryani, in as much as both involve meat, fish or vegetables and rice, cooked in a single pot, and once the cooking begins it needs to be left well alone. And now I've found a very good recipe for a seafood biryani. You can make it with whatever seafood you like, but personally I never put molluscs like clams or mussels in a dish that takes very long to cook because I don't think they taste brilliant. I suppose this is also an unusual recipe because not many people will associate biryanis with Kerala. At first glance it looks a bit involved, but it doesn't take much effort to put together – a good food processor definitely helps! This is slightly smaller than a lot of biryanis and serves four nicely. *Recipe photograph overleaf*

SERVES 4

For the seafood
800g unpeeled raw or 400g peeled tail-on raw prawns
150g firm white fish, like monkfish, sea bass, bream or John Dory, cut into 4cm x 7cm pieces
75g cleaned squid, cut into rings
Juice of 1 lime
½ tsp Kashmiri chilli powder
½ tsp salt
¼ tsp turmeric

For the spice paste
3 dried Kashmiri chillies, whole, with seeds
1 star anise
2 tsp fennel seeds
2 tsp poppy seeds
½ tsp black peppercorns
5cm piece of cinnamon stick
50g/10 cloves garlic, roughly chopped
25g/5cm ginger, roughly chopped
2 tbsp fresh or frozen grated coconut

4 tbsp (60g) ghee, coconut oil or vegetable oil
3 medium onions, finely sliced
Small handful of fresh curry leaves
1 tsp *Garam masala* (page 303)
1 tsp salt
3 tomatoes, roughly chopped

For the rice
6 green cardamom pods, lightly bruised with a rolling pin
2 Indian bay leaves
350g basmati rice, soaked in cold water for 1 hour

To finish and serve
Juice of 1 lime
25g butter
2 tbsp roughly chopped mint leaves
1 tbsp roughly chopped coriander leaves
2 tbsp cashew nuts, fried until golden
Natural yogurt or *Raita* (page 304) and *Kachumber salad* (page 305), to serve

For the seafood, peel the prawns, leaving the tail piece attached. Mix the prawns, fish and squid with the lime juice, chilli powder, salt and turmeric, then set aside.

For the spice paste, heat a frying pan over a medium heat. Add the chillies, star anise, fennel seeds, poppy seeds, peppercorns and cinnamon stick, and fry for 1–2 minutes until aromatic. Cool slightly, transfer to a spice grinder and grind to a fine powder. Put the garlic, ginger and coconut into a food processor. Add the ground spices and 100ml water and blend to a smooth paste.

Bring a large pan of salted water to the boil ready to cook the rice. Meanwhile, heat the ghee or oil in a heavy ovenproof casserole over a medium heat. Add the onions and fry for 10–15 minutes until golden, then stir in the curry leaves, garam masala, salt and tomatoes. Cook for 5 minutes until the tomatoes have softened, then add the coconut spice paste and fry for 5–7 minutes or until the sauce has darkened in colour and the oil has started to separate. Add 100ml water and stir to scrape any browned bits off the bottom of the pan; by now you should have a thick but moist paste. Keep warm over a very low heat, adding a splash of water if it becomes too dry.

Preheat the oven to 160°C/Gas 3.

For the rice, add the cardamom pods and bay leaves to the pan of boiling water. Drain the rice from its soaking water, add to the pan of boiling water, bring back to the boil and cook for 2–6 minutes. Test whether the rice is cooked by squeezing a grain between your fingers – it should be soft and break up at the edges, but stay firm in the middle. Drain (you can leave the whole spices in the rice) and assemble the biryani while the rice is still piping hot.

Spoon the still-hot spice paste out of the casserole into a bowl. Without rinsing the casserole, spoon half the hot rice over the bottom. Cover the rice with the hot spice paste, followed by the seafood and any juices, then cover with the remaining rice.

Squeeze over the lime juice, dot with butter and cover tightly with foil and a lid. Bake for 20 minutes, by which time the rice should be tender and the seafood cooked. Scatter over the mint, coriander and cashew nuts. Serve at the table in the pot, digging deep to scoop out a bit of everything for each portion, with yogurt and salad on the side.

FISH CURRY WITH BLACK CARDAMOM, CINNAMON, GREEN CHILLI AND COCONUT MILK
Fish molee

I was quite surprised to find a fish molee cooked in the Punjab. It's a dish I associate with Southeast Asia and Kerala; essentially it's just a fish curry with coconut. But Shailja Katoch's grandfather, who wrote an acclaimed book, *Cooking Delights of the Maharajas*, got the recipe from a Keralan family and it's now very much part of the Katoch household. They use the excellent freshwater fish from the rivers that flow through their considerable estate, and also from the dam, which is more of a lake. The Katochs were mentioned in a journal of Alexander the Great's, which makes them, as Ash Katoch said without a trace of arrogance, possibly the oldest family in the world. I very much enjoyed their company, and this excellent fish curry, which Shailja cooked for me on a driftwood fire on a beach on Pong Dam. It's easy to buy catfish fillet in the UK, where it's often called river cobbler. In Australia and North America it's more often known as basa. If you can't get catfish, a white fish fillet such as pouting or whiting would be fine.

SERVES 4–6

90ml mustard oil (see page 312) or vegetable oil

2 medium onions, finely sliced

2 black cardamom pods, lightly bruised with a rolling pin

4 cloves

2 x 3cm pieces of cinnamon stick

1 Indian bay leaf (optional)

20g/4 cloves garlic, cut in half lengthways

20g/4cm ginger, shredded

2 green chillies, split in half lengthways

1 tsp turmeric

1 tsp plain flour

1 tsp salt

600g river cobbler (catfish) fillets, cut into chunks

200ml coconut milk

Juice of ½–1 lime

Boiled basmati rice (page 313), to serve

Heat the oil in a heavy-based saucepan or karahi over a medium heat and fry the onions for 10 minutes until golden. Add the cardamom, cloves, cinnamon and bay leaf and fry for 1 minute, then add the garlic, ginger, green chillies and turmeric, and fry for a further minute. Stir in the flour and salt and cook for 1 minute. Add the fish pieces, pour over water just to cover and simmer for 3 minutes until the fish is part cooked. Add the coconut milk, bring back to a simmer and cook for a further 2–3 minutes, until the fish is cooked through. Sharpen with lime juice. Serve with rice.

CHETTINAD CRAB CURRY

When I arrived in Tamil Nadu from the north of India and found fabulous seafood all down the Coromandel coast, it was like I'd come home. This combination of whole crab, coconut and tamarind with curry leaves, tomatoes, chilli and spices is going on the menu at the Seafood Restaurant this summer. *Recipe photograph overleaf*

SERVES 2

1 x 750g cooked brown crab

For the coconut paste
1 tsp fennel seeds
1 tsp cumin seeds
25g fresh or frozen
   coconut flesh, blitzed
   in a food processor
   or grated

For the masala
2 tbsp vegetable oil
1 tsp fennel seeds
1 tsp fenugreek seeds

50g/10 cloves garlic,
   finely chopped
3 shallots, thinly sliced
1 medium onion, thinly sliced
10–14 fresh curry leaves
2 tsp Kashmiri chilli powder
1 tsp turmeric
4–5 tomatoes, finely chopped
200ml water
2 tbsp chopped dried kokum
1 tsp *Tamarind liquid* (page 313)
1 tbsp ground coriander
1 tsp jaggery or soft brown sugar
1 tsp salt

For the crab, break off the tail flaps and discard. Break off the claws, then take a large-bladed knife and cut them in half at the joint; crack the shells of each piece with a hammer or the back of a knife. Chop the body section in half, then gently tug on the legs to pull the body pieces away from the back shell. Use a knife as an added lever if you need to, but the body pieces should come away quite easily with the legs still attached. Turn each piece over and pick off the dead man's fingers (soft gills), then cut in half once more so you have 2 legs attached to each piece.

For the coconut paste, grind the fennel and cumin seeds, then add to a mini food processor with the coconut and a splash of water and blend to a smooth paste.

For the masala, heat the oil in a heavy-based saucepan or karahi over a medium heat, add the fennel and fenugreek seeds, garlic, shallots and onion and fry for 10 minutes until the onion is golden. Stir in the curry leaves, chilli powder and turmeric, fry for 30 seconds, then add the tomatoes. Simmer for 5–10 minutes, stirring occasionally, until the tomatoes have reduced down to a pulp. Stir in the coconut paste and fry for 2–3 minutes. Add the water, kokum, tamarind liquid, coriander, sugar and salt and bring to a boil. Add the crab, cover the pan, and cook over a high heat for 3–4 minutes until the sauce is rich and quite thick, adding a splash more water if it looks like catching on the bottom of the pan. Serve.

MUSSEL MASALA WITH COCONUT, GINGER AND GREEN CHILLIES

The Keralan Backwaters are stuffed full of good things to eat: karimeen, the very pleasant-tasting, flat, round fish prone to boniness; lots of other fish which like brackish water; shrimps; prawns the size of lobsters; and lots of clams. This dish is based on a clam masala, but I've used mussels instead as they're easier to get hold of. The Keralans like to boil their clams and then cook them again in the rich, red coconut and chilli masalas they serve them up in, a firm favourite in the toddy shops – the scruffy bars where the locals go to drink fermented coconut flower sap. I visited one such bar in the early afternoon. It's extremely rude not to down the first drink without drawing breath, and actually it was rather nice and not particularly alcoholic, but apparently as the day progresses the fermentation gets stronger and by the evening there are quite a few pissed Keralans around. Two things are banned at the toddy shops – talking politics and singing. I kept pinching myself because it reminded me so much of the Farmers' Arms in St Merryn in the early 1960s.

SERVES 2-4

1.5 kg live mussels, cleaned and debearded (discard any with broken shells or any open shells that don't close tightly when tapped firmly)
30ml coconut oil
1 tsp black mustard seeds
50g fresh or frozen coconut, grated or blitzed in a food processor
1 small onion, finely chopped
30g/6cm ginger, finely grated

20g/4 cloves garlic, finely crushed
2 green chillies, seeds removed, thinly sliced
Handful of fresh curry leaves
1 tsp fennel seeds
1 tsp ground black pepper
1 tsp *Garam masala* (page 303)
½ tsp Kashmiri chilli powder
½ tsp turmeric
1 tsp salt

Put the mussels into a large saucepan, cover with a lid and cook over a high heat, shaking the pan every now and again until all the mussels have opened and are cooked; it takes 3–4 minutes.

Heat the coconut oil in a large sturdy pan or karahi over a medium heat. Add the mustard seeds and fry for 30 seconds until they start to pop, then stir in the coconut and fry for 1 minute. Add the onion, ginger, garlic, green chillies and curry leaves and fry for a further 5 minutes.

Add the mussels and their cooking liquor to the pan, followed by the fennel seeds, black pepper, garam masala, chilli powder, turmeric and salt. Cook for a further 1–2 minutes, then serve.

MANGALORE LOBSTER MASALA

Some people feel that putting a spicy masala with a good, expensive lobster is heresy, but I disagree. While the masala in this is thick and rich with coconut, it's also subtle and accentuates the unique sweetness of lobster.

SERVES 4

For the coconut spice blend
100g fresh or frozen coconut, grated or blitzed in a food processor
4 dried Kashmiri chillies, half with seeds removed
1 tsp coriander seeds
1 tsp fenugreek seeds
½ tsp cumin seeds
Seeds of 2 green cardamom pods
1.5cm piece of cinnamon stick

For the masala
1 tbsp vegetable oil
35g onion, finely chopped
10g/2 cloves garlic, finely crushed

10g/2cm ginger, finely grated
Scant ¼ tsp turmeric
Small handful of curry leaves
100–120ml water
200ml coconut milk
½ tsp white wine vinegar
½ tsp salt
1 tbsp roughly chopped kokum, soaked in 30ml boiling water for 10 minutes, or 50ml *Tamarind liquid* (page 313)
2 x 750g cooked lobsters

To serve
A salad of peeled, sliced cucumber, dusted with salt and sprinkled with lime juice

Preheat the oven to 120°C/Gas ½. For the coconut spice blend, toast the coconut in a dry frying pan over a medium heat, stirring constantly, until golden. Transfer to a plate. In the same pan, dry-fry the chillies, coriander, fenugreek, cumin, cardamom and cinnamon for 1 minute until lightly toasted. Transfer the spices and coconut to a spice grinder and grind to a fine powder (you may need to do this in batches).

For the masala, heat the oil in a wide-bottomed saucepan or karahi over a medium heat. Add the onion and fry for 5–8 minutes, then stir in the garlic, ginger, turmeric and curry leaves and fry for 1–2 minutes. Add the coconut spice blend and 100ml water and cook, stirring occasionally, for 5–10 minutes until the masala darkens. Add a little extra water if the sauce starts to stick. Pour in the coconut milk, vinegar, salt and kokum (plus soaking liquid) or tamarind. Bring to a simmer and cook for 5–10 minutes until reduced and thick.

Cut the lobsters in half lengthways, remove the meat from the bodies and claws and set aside. Place the shells on a roasting tray in the oven to warm through. Add the lobster meat to the masala and stir gently for 2–3 minutes over a low heat. Fill the shells with the warm meat coated with the masala. Serve with cucumber salad.

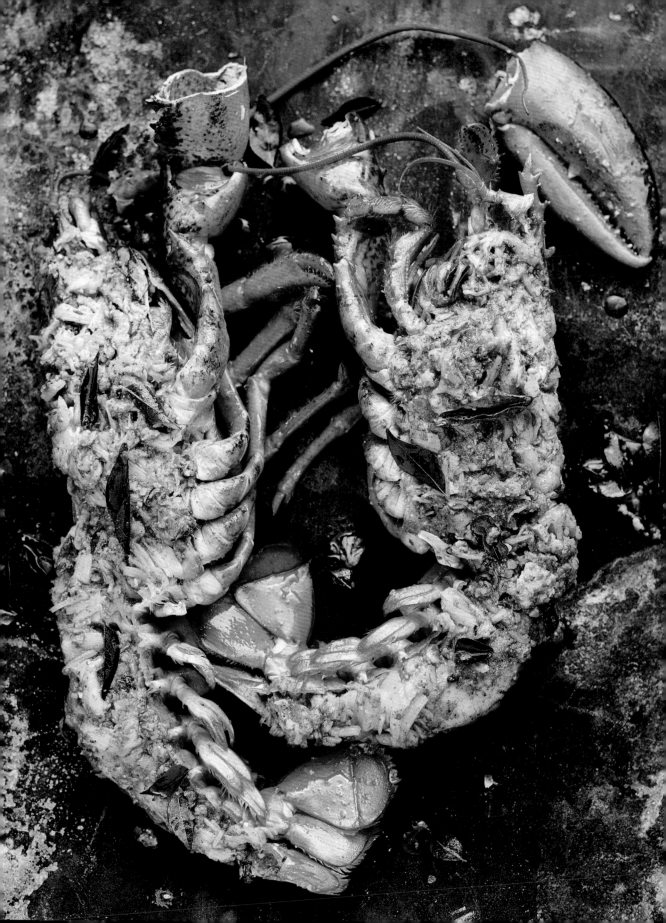

FISH IN A PARCEL WITH GREEN CHILLI, GINGER AND CORIANDER
Patra ni machi

No one in India would tell you that foil makes a good substitute for banana leaf. Instead they would insist that the leaf imparts a subtle moist quality to a dish. However, although banana leaves are getting easier to find, I didn't want anyone who couldn't get them to miss trying this excellent fish dish from Gujarat. And I urge you to buy a thermal probe; they're quite inexpensive now and they take the guesswork out. Simply cook fish until it reaches 60°C in the centre.

SERVES 6

RECIPE NOTE
If using banana leaves, warm over a flame to make them malleable. Brush the smooth side with oil then, using cotton thread, wrap the fish in the leaf and secure it.

6 x 160–180g salmon steaks
Vegetable oil

For marinating the fish
4 tbsp lime juice
　(about 2–3 limes)
1 tsp salt
¼ tsp turmeric

For the green chilli, ginger and spice paste
6 tbsp fresh or frozen coconut flesh, blitzed in a food processor or grated

3 green chillies, roughly chopped, with or without seeds according to preference
Handful of coriander leaves
Handful of mint leaves
20g/4cm ginger, chopped
20g/4 cloves garlic, chopped
½ tsp toasted ground cumin seeds
¼ tsp turmeric
½ tsp sugar
1 tbsp vegetable oil, plus extra for the foil

Put the fish steaks in a shallow dish. Mix the lime juice, salt and turmeric and, using your hands, rub this mixture over both sides of the fish (wear gloves if you don't want turmeric stains on your hands). Set aside for 15 minutes.

For the paste, put all the ingredients into a food processor and blend until fairly smooth. Rub all over the fish and leave for a further 10 minutes.

Prepare 6 squares of foil, large enough to wrap the fish in, and brush one side of each sheet with vegetable oil. Place a fish steak in the centre of each piece of foil then wrap them up to form parcels.

Place the fish parcels in one large or two smaller steamers and steam for 10 minutes or until the fish is cooked through (check one to be sure), leaving the others sealed, to be unwrapped at the table.

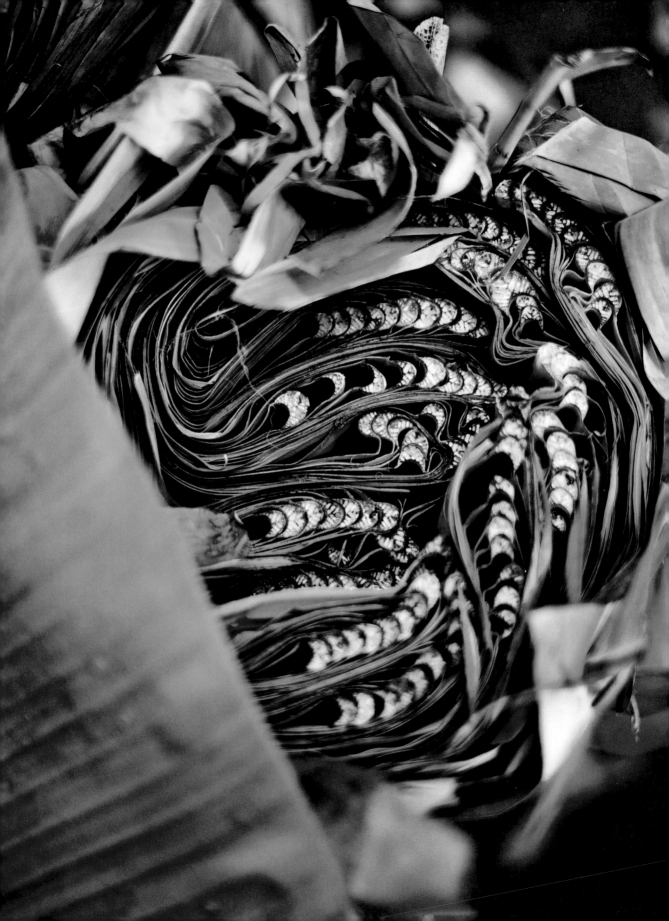

MADRAS FISH CURRY OF SNAPPER, TOMATO AND TAMARIND

I have written at some length in the main introduction about finding this curry, which I have nominated as my favourite. I've used the same fish it was cooked with on that day in Mamallapuram – snapper – but in the UK I recommend using any of the following: monkfish fillet, because you get firm slices of white, meaty fish; filleted bass, preferably a large fish, because although you'll get softer flesh it has plenty of flavour; or gurnard. I think more than anything else that this dish typifies what I was saying about really fresh fish not being ruined by a spicy curry. I can still remember the slightly oily flavour of the exquisite snapper in that dish because fish oil, when it's perfectly fresh, is very nice to eat. I always think oily fish goes well with curry anyway, particularly with the flavours of tomatoes, tamarind and curry leaves.

SERVES 4–6

60ml vegetable oil
1 tbsp yellow mustard seeds
1 large onion, finely chopped
15g/3 cloves garlic,
   finely crushed
30 fresh curry leaves
2 tsp Kashmiri chilli powder
2 tsp ground coriander
2 tsp turmeric
400g can chopped tomatoes

100ml *Tamarind liquid*
   (page 313)
2 green chillies, each sliced
   lengthways into 6 pieces,
   with seeds
1 tsp salt
700g snapper fillets,
   cut into 5cm chunks
Boiled basmati rice
   (page 313), to serve

Heat the oil in a heavy-based saucepan or karahi over a medium heat. When hot, add the mustard seeds and fry for 30 seconds, then stir in the onion and garlic and fry gently for about 10 minutes until softened and lightly golden. Add the curry leaves, chilli powder, coriander and turmeric and fry for 2 minutes, then stir in the tomatoes, tamarind liquid, green chillies and salt and simmer for about 10 minutes until rich and reduced. Add the fish, cook for a further 5 minutes or until just cooked through, and serve with plain rice.

AMRITSARI FISH

In India, unlike in the UK, they are blessed with massive rivers everywhere, so the sight of plentiful, large freshwater fish is common in markets all over the country. They treat fish as they might mutton or paneer, and quite often cook it with a lot of spicy accompaniments, which I think we would find very agreeable if we were more familiar with it. This Amritsari fish is a case in point. When I first tasted it, I knew I had to get it on the menu in the Seafood Restaurant. In India it is often made with singara – a mildly flavoured, local river fish that tastes like a white sea fish with no trace of muddy flavour. I've used farmed bream in this recipe; you could also use bass. I like the chickpea flour in the batter; it gives the fish a pleasing savouriness.

SERVES 3-6

For the fish
10g/2cm ginger, finely grated
8g/1 large clove garlic,
    finely crushed
2 tsp vegetable oil
3 x 150g fillets of sea bream,
    each cut into 2

For the batter
50g chickpea
    (gram/besan) flour
1 tsp turmeric
½ tsp salt

1 free-range egg, lightly beaten
5g/1cm ginger, finely grated
4g/1 small clove garlic,
    finely crushed
Mustard oil (see page 312)
    or vegetable oil, for
    deep frying

To serve
Pinch of *Chat masala*
    (page 303), lemon wedges,
    Green chutney (page 303),
    Kachumber salad (page 305)

For the fish, mix together the ginger, garlic and vegetable oil, then rub this over the fish fillets and leave to marinate for 15 minutes.

To make the batter, sift the chickpea flour, turmeric and salt into a bowl. Mix the egg with the ginger and garlic and 2–3 tablespoons of cold water. Whisk the liquid into the flour, adding a little more water if needed, until you have a smooth batter with the consistency of double cream.

Heat the mustard or vegetable oil in a sturdy, deep-sided pan over a medium-high heat. Drop a tiny amount of batter into the hot oil to check it's hot enough; the batter should rise and bubble. Coat the fish in the batter, carefully add to the hot oil and fry for 2–3 minutes, turning once, until golden and crisp. Remove with a slotted spoon and drain on kitchen paper. Sprinkle with a pinch of chat masala and serve with lemon wedges, green chutney and kachumber salad.

SEA BASS POLLICHATHU IN BANANA LEAF
Karimeen pollichathu

This recipe was cooked for me at a little waterside restaurant I discovered while exploring the Backwaters of Alleppey. It was in the Kainakary area of Vembanad Lake, and they cooked this dish with karimeen, which is a tasty, if rather bony, fish much prized by Keralans. I've substituted small farmed sea bass for the karimeen. And very good it is too. I've written the recipe for the fish to be steamed in foil, but it is possible to get banana leaves in the UK which, as well as keeping fish really moist, look much more appetizing.

SERVES 4

RECIPE NOTE
You'll need 4 pieces of foil large enough to wrap each fish, or 4 banana leaves. If you have leaves, use them as described on page 160.

4 whole sea bass, each weighing about 250–300g (or dabs, John Dory, plaice, flounder or lemon sole)
2 tbsp coconut oil or vegetable oil, for frying

For the marinade
2 tbsp lemon juice
1 tsp salt
½ tsp turmeric
½ tsp Kashmiri chilli powder

For the masala
50ml coconut oil or vegetable oil
1 small onion, finely sliced
1 small tomato, finely sliced
1 tsp ground black pepper
1 tsp *Garam masala* (page 303)
1 tsp Kashmiri chilli powder
½ tsp turmeric
1 tsp salt
Handful of fresh curry leaves
2 green chillies, finely chopped, with seeds

In a shallow dish mix together the marinade ingredients, add the fish and turn to coat. Set aside while you make the masala.

Heat the oil in a heavy-based pan or karahi over a medium heat. Add the onion and fry for 10 minutes until softened and golden brown, then stir in the tomato, spices and salt and cook for a further 5 minutes. Stir in the curry leaves and green chillies and remove from the heat. Preheat the oven to 200°C/Gas 6.

Heat the coconut or vegetable oil in a large frying pan over a high heat and fry the fish for 1–2 minutes on each side to brown slightly, but not to cook the fish through.

Open out the 4 pieces of foil or banana leaves and place a spoonful of the masala in the centre of each, spreading it out a little. Place a fish on top then spread the remaining masala over each fish. Fold the foil or banana leaves into parcels and place on a baking tray. Cook in the oven for 10 minutes. Unwrap the parcels at the table to serve.

HOT SMOKED SALMON KEDGEREE

There's a view about that Indians aren't really interested in Anglo-Indian cuisine such as kedgeree. I may have been mixing in some rather elevated circles but I didn't find that to be the case. Indeed, I've had several interesting conversations with people recalling with great nostalgia the dishes served at station restaurants in the 1950s and 1960s, when the sort of food the British loved was still on the menu. I've included a few recipes in the book that these days are perhaps more at home in England than India. This is the perfect dish for hot smoked salmon.

SERVES 6

1 tbsp fennel seeds
1½ tsp cumin seeds
½ tsp turmeric
¼ tsp Kashmiri chilli powder
350g basmati rice
600ml water
1 tsp salt

4 free-range eggs
50g butter
350g hot smoked salmon,
   skinned and roughly flaked
Large handful of parsley,
   chopped
1 tbsp lemon juice

Place half the fennel seeds and half the cumin seeds into a dry frying pan over a medium heat and fry for about 1 minute until fragrant. Stir in the turmeric and chilli powder, then tip into a spice grinder and reduce to a powder.

Put the rice and water into a saucepan with the salt and bring to the boil over a high heat. Reduce the heat to low, cover and simmer for 8–10 minutes until all the water has been absorbed and the rice is just tender. After 8 minutes, check by squeezing a grain between the fingers. You want rice that is soft on the outside, but still firm within. When done, stir gently with a fork to separate the grains.

Put the eggs in a small saucepan of simmering water and boil for 7 minutes, then drain and cover with cold water until cool enough to handle. Remove the shells and cut the eggs into quarters.

Melt the butter in a heavy-based saucepan or karahi over a medium heat, add the remaining whole fennel seeds and cumin seeds and fry for 30 seconds, then add the ground spices and hot rice and fry for 5 minutes until steaming hot. Gently fold in the salmon, parsley, lemon juice and eggs, and serve at once.

BOMBAY SALMON MASALA CURRY
Meen masala

This is a quick and simple dish to make, and very rewarding in that there's a lot of flavour for not a great deal of effort. In my opinion it's the perfect curry for farmed salmon. In India they tend to cook all their fish absolutely right through, but it pays to cook the salmon in this dish only until it's still soft and pink in the centre.

SERVES 4

For the coconut spice paste
1 tsp coriander seeds
1 tsp cumin seeds
1 tsp black mustard seeds
1 tsp fenugreek seeds
½ tsp turmeric
100g fresh or frozen coconut
   flesh, grated or chopped
3 fresh red chillies, seeds
   removed, roughly chopped
15g/3 cloves garlic,
   roughly chopped
50ml water

For the rest of the dish
2 tbsp vegetable oil
1 medium onion, finely chopped
200g vine-ripened
   tomatoes, chopped
2 fresh green chillies,
   with seeds, sliced in
   quarters lengthways
15g/3cm ginger, finely shredded
100ml *Tamarind liquid*
   (page 313)
1 tsp salt
600g salmon fillet, skin on,
   cut into 2cm-thick slices
Boiled basmati rice
   (page 313), to serve

For the coconut spice paste, tip the coriander seeds, cumin seeds, mustard seeds and fenugreek seeds into a spice grinder and blend to a powder. (Or use a pestle and mortar.) Transfer to a mini food processor with the turmeric, coconut, red chillies, garlic and water. Blend to a coarse paste.

In a large sturdy pan or karahi, heat the oil over a medium heat and fry the onion for 10 minutes until softened and golden. Stir in the coconut spice paste and cook for 5 minutes then stir in the tomatoes, green chillies, ginger, tamarind liquid and salt. Bring to a simmer, add the salmon and cook for 5 minutes, stirring gently once or twice, until the salmon is cooked. Serve with rice.

COD CURRY
Meen kulambu

As I watched this dish being cooked in Pondicherry, I thought it was the perfect recipe for our own cod; you could also try it with pollock, haddock or hake. Another simple, fresh and fragrant curry from southern India, and, as I'm rather too fond of saying, if we could get fish dishes like this anywhere, everyone would love fish.

SERVES 4–6

For the paste
1 small onion, chopped
1 small tomato, chopped
80g fresh or frozen coconut, grated or chopped
30g/6 cloves garlic, peeled
9 dried Kashmiri chillies, stalks snipped off
1 tbsp black peppercorns
1½ tsp salt

For the fish
50ml vegetable oil
1 tsp black mustard seeds

1 tsp urid dal (husked)
2 tsp turmeric
150ml water
600g cod fillet (or pollock, haddock or hake), cut into 4cm slices
Handful of fresh curry leaves
Handful of fresh coriander leaves

To serve
Boiled basmati rice (page 313) and *Chapatis* (page 306)

Put all the paste ingredients in a mini food processor and blend to a thick paste, adding a splash of water if needed.

Heat the oil in a heavy-based saucepan or karahi over a medium heat. Add the mustard seeds and urid dal and fry for 30 seconds, then add the paste and the turmeric, and fry for 2–3 minutes until fragrant. Add the water, bring to the boil then add the cod. Cook for 5 minutes, or until cooked through, occasionally shaking the pan gently to distribute the heat (avoid using a utensil to stir as the fish is delicate and will break up).

Finally add the curry leaves and coriander to the pan and serve with rice and Indian bread.

YESTERDAY'S FISH CURRY

This recipe comes from a book called *The Suriani Kitchen*. The author, Lathika George, who took me on a fascinating trip round a frenetic market just outside Cochin, is an authority on Keralan cooking. She explained that it's called 'yesterday's curry' because everybody thinks it's much better the next day. I came across the same curry all over the place – in a kitchen so smoky I couldn't stay in there for more than a minute at a time, where it featured a giant kingfish head; at the house where I was filmed cooking lots of the recipes in the book, where the cook Mallika had one on every day; and in the hotel where we all stayed for about two weeks. The hotel was the sort of place of air-conditioned comfort where you go quietly mad for want of the warp and weft of everyday Indian life; we had to leave at six o'clock every morning to work a twelve-hour day in enervating humidity. As a matter of interest, I first tasted this dish years ago in a restaurant in central London called Rasa Samudra, and then, as now, was taken by its spicy redness and the smoky flavour and souring effect of kokum. As if it wasn't hard enough to get hold of kokum anyway, now you need to make sure it's the smoky sort – but don't worry, tamarind is nearly as good.

SERVES 4–6

60ml vegetable oil
1 medium onion, thinly sliced
15g/3cm piece ginger,
    finely grated
50g/10 cloves garlic,
    half crushed to a paste,
    half thinly sliced
8 fresh curry leaves
1 tbsp Kashmiri chilli powder
½ tsp ground turmeric
1 tbsp ground coriander
½ tsp toasted ground fenugreek
1 tbsp rice flour or plain flour

2 tomatoes, sliced
2 tbsp sliced smoked kokum,
    washed and soaked in 100ml
    boiling water for 15 minutes,
    or 50ml *Tamarind liquid*
    (page 313)
500ml water
1½ tsp salt
1 tsp sugar
500g salmon fillet,
    cut into 3cm chunks
1 tsp coconut oil, warmed
    to its liquid state, to finish

Heat the oil in a heavy-based pan or karahi over a medium heat, add the onion and fry for 5 minutes until softened. Add the ginger, crushed and sliced garlic and curry leaves and fry for 2 minutes. Stir in the chilli powder, ground spices and flour and a splash of water, and cook for 2 minutes. Stir in the tomatoes, kokum (plus soaking water) or tamarind, water, salt and sugar and simmer for 5 minutes. Add the salmon and cook for a further 5 minutes. Remove from the heat, drizzle with coconut oil and serve.

BENGALI MUSTARDY FISH CURRY

Kewpies is probably the most famous restaurant in Calcutta, thanks to the owner, Rakhi Das Gupta's mother, Minakshie, who wrote the charming *Bengal Cookbook*, a collection of recipes gathered while she was running the restaurant. In the book she notes that it is customary in Bengal to serve a meal as a number of courses, whereas in the rest of India, of course, everything is served at the same time. I had a lunch there of eight courses, after which we repaired to the kitchen where Rakhi conducted the cooking of the Bengal curry. As is usually the case, the actual cooking is done by a chef, in this case a very handsome woman whose skill at grinding the all-essential mustard seeds on a big stone slab with a round roller was prodigious. Fish curries from Bengal take some getting used to because of the pungency of the mustard in them, but I ended up liking them a great deal. One thing to note in all fish dishes here is that they season the fish with salt and turmeric and fry it quickly before going on to cook the curry with the mustard and chillies. The finished curry is quite thin but very well flavoured. The mustard oil is an important element in this dish, and can't be substituted with vegetable oil as in other dishes.

SERVES 4

2 ½ tbsp black mustard seeds
½ tsp turmeric
¼ tsp Kashmiri chilli powder
3 tbsp mustard oil (see page 312)
4 x 125g cod steaks

1 tsp salt
6–8 green chillies,
  with seeds, each sliced
  lengthways into 8 strips
200g peeled raw prawns

Put the mustard seeds in a mini food processor and add 2 tablespoons of water. Blend for a minute then add another 2 tablespoons of water and continue blending until the seeds start to break up (this can take a minute or two of persistent blending; add more water if you're having trouble). Keep blending until you have a rough paste that resembles wholegrain mustard, adding a splash more water if needed. Mix the mustard paste with half the turmeric, the chilli powder and 500ml water.

Heat the mustard oil in a large, shallow pan over a medium-high heat. Season the fish with the salt and remaining turmeric and fry for a minute or two on each side until lightly coloured but not cooked through, then take off the heat.

Strain the mustard liquid through a fine sieve into a clean pan, add the chillies, and bring to a simmer over a medium heat for 3 minutes, then add the fish and prawns and simmer for 5 minutes until they are cooked through. Serve.

TANDOORI FISH WITH NAANS
Ajwaini fish tikka

Any meat or fish from the tandoor oven cries out to be accompanied by my favourite bread in India, also from the tandoor: naan. The pleasure to me of wrapping a piece of roasted spiced monkfish in a slightly charred, garlic butter naan is like a really good steak with crisp chips and a glass of wine. So it was very fortunate that this excellent recipe, which comes from the Royal Heritage Haveli, my hotel in Jaipur, was served with exquisite naans. *Recipe photograph overleaf*

SERVES 4

For the fish
Juice of ½ lemon
1 tsp Kashmiri chilli powder
1 tsp turmeric
½ tsp salt
500g monkfish fillet,
   cut into 5cm chunks

For the tandoori paste
1 tsp fennel seeds
1 tsp caraway seeds
½ tsp Kashmiri chilli powder
½ tsp salt

50g natural yogurt
30g cashew nuts
15g/3cm ginger,
   roughly chopped
10g/2 cloves garlic,
   roughly chopped
1 tsp beetroot powder
   (for colour; optional)

To serve
Pinch of *Chat masala*
   (page 303), *Garlic butter
   naans* (page 306)

Preheat the oven to its highest setting. Mix together the lemon juice, chilli powder, turmeric and salt. Rub this all over the fish pieces and set aside for 5 minutes.

For the tandoori paste, put the fennel seeds, caraway seeds, chilli powder and salt into a spice grinder and blend to a powder. Transfer the ground spices to a mini food processor with the yogurt, cashew nuts, ginger, garlic and beetroot powder, if using, and blend to a paste.

Rub the paste all over the marinated fish, then arrange the fish on a wire rack over a roasting tin and place on the top shelf of the oven. Cook for 5 minutes, or until just cooked through. Sprinkle with chat masala and serve with garlic butter naans.

FISH FRY WITH GARLIC, CUMIN AND KASHMIRI CHILLI

As with all my cookery books, when this one comes out I'll have to find a couple of dishes to do impromptu demonstrations of, and this spicy fried fish from the Alleppey Backwaters in Kerala will be one of them. It's so simple to do that I can be quickly frying it while talking to a presenter about tuk-tuks, elephants and *Slumdog Millionaire*. It goes without saying it is totally delicious.

SERVES 4

For the marinade
15g/3 cloves garlic,
   finely crushed
15g/3cm ginger, finely grated
2 tsp lemon juice
2 tsp cornflour
2 tsp Kashmiri chilli powder
1 tsp ground black pepper
1 tsp ground cumin
½ tsp turmeric
1 tsp salt

For the fish
4 whole dabs, John Dory,
   plaice, flounder or lemon
   sole (each weighing
   about 250g–300g)
50ml coconut oil
   or vegetable oil

To serve
Kachumber salad (page 305)
   and lime wedges

In a bowl mix together all the marinade ingredients.

Make 4 shallow cuts across each fish on each side. Rub with the marinade and leave for 10 minutes. Heat the oil in a large frying pan over a medium heat and fry the fish for 4 minutes on each side.

Serve with kachumber salad and lime wedges.

PONDICHERRY MACKEREL FISH FRY

Curious to think that this very simple mackerel dish cooked in a humble fisherman's cottage in Pondicherry will probably end up as a starter at the Seafood Restaurant in Padstow, it was that good. Mrs Prabhe, who cooked it, would have been, in a different world, another Angela Hartnett. She was simply a very good cook. This is just what you should do with fish: keep it simple, albeit spicy. *Recipe photograph overleaf*

SERVES 4-8

125g natural yogurt
50g/10 cloves garlic,
    finely crushed
2 tbsp Kashmiri
    chilli powder
1 tsp salt
Juice of ½ lime

50–100ml water
8 fillets of fresh mackerel
3 tbsp vegetable oil
Handful of coriander
    leaves, chopped
Pinch of salt
Lime wedges, to serve

In a large bowl mix together the yogurt, garlic, chilli powder, salt and lime juice, then stir in enough water to give the consistency of double cream (the amount will depend on the brand of yogurt and the juiciness of the lime).

Add the mackerel fillets and turn them over to coat in the yogurt mixture. Set aside to marinate for 5–10 minutes.

Heat the oil in a large frying pan over a medium heat. When the oil is hot, fry the mackerel in batches for 3 minutes on each side.

Sprinkle with coriander leaves and salt, and serve with lime wedges.

MURGH

...spicy and creamy chicken curries, fragrant rice dishes and a little roast duck

How many chickens can you fit in a tuk-tuk? I only ask this because we had a bit of a wager running among the film crew while filming in India about how many cages of chickens, a tad cruelly squeezed in together, you could fit into the small three-wheeler vehicles that are such a triumph of practical engineering design. I think the record was thirteen but that was slightly cheating because they'd managed to fit some on the roof too. Chicken shops in Indian cities are a bit of a shock to Western sentiment. In India you wouldn't think of buying a chicken that wasn't still alive minutes before you made your purchase. And the slaughter and butchery is done on an old wooden block right next to where the chickens are looking on disconcertedly. But I'm afraid to say that we human beings are ultimately a bit callous. See it once or twice you're a bit shocked; after the fourth time, well, it's what they do. And the reality of it is that chickens do taste really good in India.

I remember the first time I ate tandoori chicken in India was in Goa, and it always came with delicious garlic butter naan breads, cooked in the same charcoal oven as the chicken, and peeled cucumber salads just sprinkled with lime juice and salt, and I was convinced I'd never tasted anything so addictively delicious in my life. When I finally got to see the chickens being marinated in the kitchen I was quite surprised to see how small and scrawny they were. Back in England, armed with the same recipe, I made it with supermarket free-range chicken and it was lovely but it didn't have that spicy spareness of Indian murgh. Then I tried poussins and they gave much more of the Indian taste – so you have a choice.

One thing I find very hard to understand is that they don't go for duck in India. I made the mistake of asking someone in Rajasthan why they don't serve duck and they said, 'No water.' But there's plenty of water in Bengal and on the plains of the Punjab. Thankfully in the Backwaters of Kerala they do rear ducks and duck roast is a very popular dish. Thinking of those Backwaters, and where we ended up filming a lot of the recipes in this book, I'm reminded of a couple of ducks that Ashok our host had just bought, which he kept on strings tied to their hutch. I thought it was a bit cruel but he said you have to do that for a couple of days so they remember where they live, and after he let them go they did stay in the lagoon in front of the house very close to each other. Ducks make perfect couples, and my wife Sarah called them Marcus and Florence.

ROCKY'S CHICKEN KORMA

One of the questions I constantly asked myself in India was whether I could get food like this back in the UK. More often than not the answer was probably no, and with this korma the answer was emphatically no. Lucknow, with its history of Nawab rulers, is famous for the finesse of its dishes, and Rocky Mohan's korma carries on that tradition. I had the most fabulous day cooking with him and his wife Rekha, a very successful marriage I would say. I asked her how long they'd been married – fifty, no maybe a hundred years, she said! The black cardamom added at the end of cooking is an essential flavour in this particular dish.

SERVES 4-6

1 x 1.5kg chicken, jointed into 8 pieces, or 1.5kg chicken pieces, skinned

For the coconut paste
125g fresh or frozen coconut flesh, chopped or grated
50g blanched almonds, roughly chopped
5 tsp white poppy seeds

For the masala
2 medium onions, roughly chopped
50g ghee or vegetable oil

6 cloves
6 green cardamom pods, lightly bruised with a rolling pin
3cm piece of cinnamon stick
1 tsp salt
½–¾ tsp Kashmiri chilli powder
200ml water
125ml thick Greek-style yogurt mixed with 125ml water
3 black cardamom pods, seeds only, finely ground
2 tbsp raisins, soaked in 4 tbsp boiling water for about 10 minutes, drained

For the coconut paste, blend the coconut, almonds and poppy seeds together in a mini food processor to a paste, adding enough hot water to give a silken texture.

For the masala, blend the onions in a mini food processor to a paste, adding a splash of water if needed. Heat the ghee in a sturdy, deep-sided pan over a medium heat, add the cloves, green cardamom and cinnamon stick and fry for 30 seconds. Stir in the onion paste and salt and fry for 10 minutes until any liquid has evaporated and the onions are softened and translucent, but not coloured. Stir in the chilli powder, then add the chicken pieces to the pan and fry for 10 minutes to brown slightly. Add the water and the coconut paste, bring to a simmer and cook for a further 10 minutes.

Take the pan off the heat, stir in the yogurt mixture, then return to a gentle heat and bring to a simmer. Cook, uncovered, for 30 minutes, adding a little water if it starts to stick, until the chicken is cooked through and the masala thick and rich. Stir in the ground black cardamom, scatter with the raisins and serve.

CHICKEN PASSANDA

As the somewhat disappointed recipient of various chicken passandas in British Indian restaurants, I was keen to try the real thing in Lucknow, where the dish, a typical Mughal creation, originated. Passanda in Urdu means 'favourite one', which refers to the fact that it was always made with special cuts of meat. In this case I've used chicken breasts. I soon realized that the yogurt- and almond-flavoured sauce should be so reduced that it clings to the chicken, and it should be very mild, fragrant with cardamom, ginger, coriander and cinnamon and sprinkled with toasted, flaked almonds.

SERVES 4

3 tbsp (15g) ghee
 or vegetable oil
5cm piece of cinnamon stick
2 green cardamom pods, lightly
 bruised with a rolling pin
1 small onion, finely chopped
15g/3cm ginger, finely grated
15g/3 cloves garlic,
 finely crushed
1 tsp ground coriander
½ tsp turmeric
½ tsp Kashmiri chilli powder

4 small skinless chicken
 breasts, each cut in half
200g Greek-style yogurt
2 tbsp ground almonds
1 tsp salt
100ml water

To finish
Handful of flaked
 almonds, toasted
Handful of fresh coriander
 leaves, chopped

Heat the ghee or oil in a large sturdy pan or karahi over a medium heat, add the cinnamon and cardamom and fry for 30 seconds, then add the onion and fry for 10 minutes until golden brown. Stir in the ginger and garlic and fry for 2–3 minutes, then stir in the ground coriander, turmeric and chilli powder and fry for 30 seconds.

Add the chicken and stir well, then add the yogurt, ground almonds, salt and water. Bring to a simmer, reduce the heat slightly and simmer gently for 15–20 minutes until reduced to a thick, rich, almost dry sauce that coats the chicken.

Scatter over the toasted almonds and coriander and serve.

TANDOORI CHICKEN

Tandoori brings up the vexed issue of food colouring, rather as paella does. In India they normally use it, but here we worry about it. I feel that as I don't eat it very often then it's not going to harm me, so I do add a drop or two of red and yellow. But I've now noticed that in India they will also use beetroot powder as a colour, or ratan jot (cockscomb flower), which also gives the distinctive red colour to rogan josh. Both beetroot powder and ratan jot can be found in the UK.

SERVES 4

1 x 1.5kg chicken, jointed
   into 8 pieces, or 1.5kg
   chicken pieces, skinned

For the first marinade
Juice of 2 limes
1 tsp Kashmiri chilli powder
1 tsp salt

For the second marinade
50g natural yogurt
50g double cream

20g/4 cloves garlic,
   roughly chopped
25g/5cm ginger,
   roughly chopped
1 tsp *Garam masala*
   (page 303)
1 tsp turmeric
¾ tsp ground cumin
½ tsp beetroot powder
   (for colour; optional)
Pinch of *Chat masala*
   (page 303), to finish

For the first marinade, mix the lime juice, chilli and salt in a large bowl. Add the chicken pieces and rub in the marinade. Cover and transfer to the fridge to marinate for 1 hour.

For the second marinade, put all the ingredients apart from the chat masala into a mini food processor. Blend until smooth, then add this to the marinated chicken and stir well to coat. Cover and transfer to the fridge to marinate for 4 hours.

Preheat the oven to 240°C/Gas 9 (or 220°C if your oven doesn't go that high). Thread the chicken on to lightly oiled metal skewers (you can put more than one piece per skewer, but leave space between them), then suspend the skewers above a roasting tin. Alternatively, place them on a wire rack over a roasting tin. Roast for 30–40 minutes or until lightly charred in places and cooked through. Sprinkle with chat masala and serve.

CHICKEN PICKLE

This is often taken by travellers on long journeys and eaten with parathas. I've noticed in many countries that meat has been cooked in this way as a means of preserving it since well before the days of refrigeration. The great thing about this dish is the hot mustard oil spiced with asafoetida, garlic and ginger. Pickle stalls dot the road from Punjab into Himachal Pradesh at Dharampur, en route to Shimla. These meaty pickles were made with game before hunting became illegal. *Recipe photograph overleaf*

SERVES 4

500g skinless, boneless chicken thighs, cut into 2cm pieces
1 tsp red chilli flakes
½ tsp turmeric
1½ tsp salt
40g/8 cloves garlic, crushed
50g ginger, finely grated

For the spice mix
½ tsp fenugreek seeds
1¼ tsp black mustard seeds
1¼ tsp fennel seeds
1 tsp *Garam masala* (page 303)

To finish
300ml mustard oil (see page 312) or vegetable oil
2 medium onions, thinly sliced
1 tsp salt
Pinch of asafoetida
40g/8 cloves garlic, finely chopped
50g ginger, finely chopped
150ml white wine vinegar

To serve
Parathas (page 306)

Mix the chicken with the chilli flakes, turmeric, salt, garlic and ginger. Leave to marinate for an hour.

For the spice mix, fry the fenugreek, mustard and fennel seeds in a dry frying pan for a minute or two until aromatic, stirring all the time. Cool slightly then tip into a spice grinder and blend to a fine powder. Combine with the garam masala.

Heat the oil in a sturdy pan or karahi over a medium heat until hot but not smoking. Add the onions and fry for 10–15 minutes, stirring constantly until deep golden brown. Remove with a slotted spoon and set aside. Keep the oil in the pan hot.

Pat the chicken dry with kitchen paper. Carefully, as it might spit, fry in batches in the same oil for 3–4 minutes, or until cooked through. Remove with a slotted spoon and set aside.

Add the asafoetida to the oil, followed by the spice mix, the garlic and ginger and fry for 2–3 minutes. Remove from the heat and carefully pour in the vinegar. Return to the heat, bring to a simmer then stir in the fried chicken and onions and cook, uncovered, for 3–4 minutes. Serve rolled up in parathas.

CHICKEN AND APRICOT CURRY WITH POTATO STRAWS
Sali murghi

This Parsee dish uses jaggery, soft apricots and vinegar for a really successful balance of sweet and sour. The crisp fried potatoes add crunch.

SERVES 4

For the sali
(matchstick potatoes)
250g chip potatoes such as
Maris Piper or Sebago,
peeled, cut into matchsticks
or coarsely grated, soaked
in cold water for 15 minutes
Vegetable oil, for deep frying
1–2 tsp salt

For the curry
3 tbsp vegetable oil
6 black peppercorns
5 cloves
2 green cardamom pods, lightly
bruised with a rolling pin
2 dried Kashmiri chillies
4cm piece of cinnamon stick

1 medium onion, finely chopped
100g tomatoes, finely chopped
1 tsp salt
20g/4cm ginger, finely grated
15g/3 cloves garlic, crushed
1½ tsp Kashmiri chilli powder
1 tsp ground cumin
1 tsp ground coriander
1 tsp Garam masala (page 303)
½ tsp turmeric
1kg chicken, jointed into
8 pieces, or 1kg chicken
pieces, skinned
2 tsp jaggery or soft brown sugar
150g 'ready-to-eat' soft
dried apricots
3 tbsp white wine vinegar
Handful of coriander, chopped

Drain the potatoes and dry on kitchen paper. Heat the vegetable oil in a deep pan over a medium heat until hot (or heat a deep-fat fryer to 180°C) and deep-fry the potatoes in batches until crisp and golden. Drain on kitchen paper and season with salt.

For the curry, heat the oil in a heavy-based pan or karahi over a medium heat. Add the whole spices and fry for a minute until fragrant, then add the onion and fry for 10 minutes until softened and golden. Stir in the tomatoes and salt and simmer for 2–3 minutes, then add the ginger, garlic, chilli powder, cumin, coriander, garam masala and turmeric and cook for a minute.

Add the chicken pieces to the pan and cook, stirring, for 2–3 minutes until well coated with the spice mixture, then add the jaggery, apricots, vinegar and enough water just to cover. Bring to the boil, lower the heat, cover the pan with a lid and simmer for 30–40 minutes, or until the chicken is cooked through and tender, and the sauce reduced to a rich, thick consistency. Heap the potato sticks on top, and scatter with coriander.

JOY
BASMATI RICE
76/
for processing our products.
Maximum retail price:
fluff with a fork and serve hot.

CHICKEN PULAO

This is a lovely, homely pulao, very easy to make. I've cooked dishes like it in Turkey that had clearly come from Iran. Mrs Mohinder Kaur Ghuman, whose recipe this is, was a wonderful 82-year-old. She used to run a restaurant (a dhaba) in rural Punjab, and had just won a competition for home cooks. I had heard she used to keep a gun behind the counter in the dhaba, and she confirmed it. I have no doubt she would have used it on unruly customers when necessary. You could imagine her as the landlady of a pub in Liverpool in the good old days.

SERVES 4

For the stock
2 medium onions, roughly chopped
1 bulb of garlic (about 40g), cloves peeled and roughly chopped
70g ginger, roughly chopped
1 tbsp fennel seeds
6 cloves
3 black cardamom pods, lightly bruised with a rolling pin
8 green cardamom pods, lightly bruised with a rolling pin
2 x 4cm pieces cinnamon stick
2 Indian bay leaves
⅛ tsp grated nutmeg

3 dried Kashmiri chillies, split in half
1.75 litres water
8 chicken thighs on the bone, skinned

For the rice
300g basmati rice
3 tbsp vegetable oil
2 medium onions, diced
1 tsp salt
1 tsp *Garam masala* (page 303)

To serve
Yogurt or *Raita* (page 304) and *Kachumber salad* (page 305)

Put all the stock ingredients, apart from the chicken, into a large pan, bring almost to the boil then lower the heat and simmer, uncovered, for 20 minutes. Add the chicken, simmer for a further 20 minutes or until it is cooked through and tender, then turn off the heat and leave to cool in the stock. Strain, reserving both the chicken and liquid and discarding the whole spices.

Wash the rice thoroughly, cover with cold water and soak for 15 minutes. Heat the oil in a heavy-based saucepan or karahi over a medium-high heat and fry the onions for 10 minutes until golden. Add the cooked chicken, salt and garam masala, and cook for 2–3 minutes. Drain the rice and add it to the pan, stirring gently for 1 minute to coat the grains. Pour over enough of the stock to cover the rice by 3cm, topping up with water if needed. Bring to a simmer then reduce the heat to its lowest setting, cover the pan with foil and a lid and cook, without uncovering, for 10 minutes, by which time the rice should have absorbed all the stock and be tender. Turn the heat off and leave to rest, covered, for 10 minutes. Serve with yogurt or raita and salad.

SOUR BERRY CHICKEN PULAO

I worry that my introductions are more about the extraordinary circumstances for acquiring the recipes than my enthusiasm for the dishes themselves. Let me say immediately that this chicken pulao is made wonderful by the addition of the small sour Iranian berries called barberries or zereshk. It just so happened that the Britannia restaurant in Mumbai, specializing in Parsee cooking and one of a sadly dwindling number of Irani restaurants, was also such fun. When you arrive there's a tabby cat sitting on the till with a notice saying, 'Beware, I scratch.' Then the 92-year-old owner Boman Kohinoor comes and sits down at your table to tell you what a shame it is that the British left India and how much he cares for the Queen. They sell bottles of soft drinks I've not come across since the early 1960s. The motto of the restaurant is: 'There is no love greater than the love of eating.'

SERVES 6

RECIPE NOTE
If you're going to use a whole 1.5kg chicken, then joint into thighs, drumsticks and breasts. Cut each breast into three and whack each thigh in two. You want twelve portions in total.

1 x 1.5kg chicken, jointed (see note), or 6 chicken thighs and/or drumsticks, plus 2 large breasts each cut into 3 pieces, skinned

For the marinade
1 tsp Kashmiri chilli powder
½ tsp turmeric
2 tsp salt
20g/4cm ginger, finely grated
20g/4 cloves garlic, finely crushed
2 tsp lime juice

For the pulao
3 tbsp (15g) ghee
10 black peppercorns
3cm piece of cinnamon stick
6 green cardamom pods, bruised
2 Indian bay leaves
1 blade mace
1 medium onion, sliced
400g basmati rice
25g dried barberries (or sour cherries or dried blueberries)
750ml water
Pinch of saffron soaked in 2 tbsp warm milk for 15 minutes
55g cashew nuts fried in ghee until golden, to finish

Combine all the marinade ingredients, add the chicken pieces, toss to coat well then set aside to marinade for 30 minutes.

Heat the ghee in a karahi or heavy-based saucepan over a medium heat, then fry the peppercorns, cinnamon, cardamom, bay leaves and mace for 1 minute. Add the onion and fry until light golden brown. Add the chicken and its marinade and cook for 10 minutes. Add the rice and two-thirds of the barberries, stir for 30 seconds, then add the water. Bring to the boil, reduce the heat to low-medium, cover tightly with a lid and cook for 15 minutes. Add the saffron milk and remaining barberries, cover again and rest for 5 minutes off the heat. Scatter with cashews and serve.

CHICKEN VINDAIL

This comes from Pondicherry, the city south of Chennai that was a French base for 300 years, reflected in many of the recipes. There's not a lot of French influence in this one though, apart for the title 'vindail', which means 'containing vinegar' and is the French word for vindaloo. Lourdes Tirouvanziam-Louis's recipe contains a small amount of vinegar stirred in at the end, and that's it as far as French influence goes. But she was keen to point out that it was wine vinegar and not any of your toddy stuff from Goa or Kerala. She cooked this for me in her tiny apartment while her adoring husband, a recently retired doctor, looked on. It was a very good dish and she was a precise and informative cook, explaining the reason for every stage in the cooking – tempering the whole spices for 1 minute until fragrant, frying the onions for 10–15 minutes until softened and golden brown, the gentle heating of the ground spices added next. She said Indians don't care for the smell of raw meat and fish, and so fish fillets are rubbed with salt and turmeric before cooking. She told me that she would never taste food while she was cooking, thinking it to be unhygienic. And I subsequently found that if anyone did taste something they would drip a little on to the palm of their hand. All this enhanced my sense of this curry's specialness.

SERVES 4–6

2 tbsp vegetable oil
2cm piece of cinnamon stick
1 clove
1 star anise
2 medium onions, chopped
50g/10 cloves garlic, crushed
1 tbsp ground cumin
2 tsp Kashmiri chilli powder
½ tsp toasted ground fenugreek
½ tsp turmeric
1 tsp salt
500g tomatoes,
    roughly sliced
1kg chicken thighs and
    drumsticks, on the
    bone, skinned
1 tbsp white wine vinegar
1 tsp sugar

Heat the oil in a heavy-based saucepan or karahi over a medium heat and add the cinnamon, clove and star anise, and fry for 1 minute until fragrant. Add the onions and fry for 10–15 minutes until softened and golden brown. Stir in the garlic and cumin and fry for another 2 minutes, then add the chilli powder, fenugreek, turmeric and salt and fry for 30 seconds. Add the tomatoes to the pan and cook for a further 5 minutes until they start to break down.

Add the chicken and stir everything together, then cover the pan with a lid and cook for 35 minutes, adding a splash of water if it starts to stick to the bottom. Stir in the vinegar and sugar and cook, uncovered, for 5 minutes or until the chicken is completely cooked through. Serve.

ROAST CHICKEN WITH CINNAMON AND NUTMEG, WITH A PORK, CARDAMOM AND CASHEW NUT STUFFING AND SPICE-SCENTED GRAVY

This is not an authentic Indian dish. It's something I made up to bring some of the flavours of India to a roast chicken. I went out to the country estate of a family who had turned their Rajput palace in Deogarh near Ajmer into a hotel very much on the Rajasthan baby-boomer circuit. Mrs Prabha Singh, the head of the family, cooked a beautiful lal maas, a red chilli lamb (page 234), for us to film, and a khad murgh, a chicken in a wrapping of chapati, was gently cooking in a covered pit fired up with cow dung. Due to a misunderstanding, the khad murgh was well underway when we arrived so we couldn't film it being made, but I did have a chance to taste it and, while I thought it too complicated to reproduce here, I was so overwhelmed by the fragrant flavours that I thought it would work very well as a simple British roast chicken dish, and damn me if I wasn't right. *Recipe photograph overleaf*

SERVES 4-6

1 x 1.5kg chicken
Juice of 1 lemon
2 tsp mild paprika
1 tsp salt
30g softened butter

For the stuffing
100g cashew nuts
1–2 tbsp boiled water
1 tsp ground cinnamon
½ tsp ground cardamom
  (seeds from 15 green pods)
¼ tsp ground nutmeg
¼ tsp salt
65g natural yogurt
100g pork mince

For the gravy
1 heaped tsp plain flour
350ml chicken stock

To serve
Roast potatoes, or try my
  *Spiced roast potatoes
  and onions* (page 306)

Sit the chicken in a roasting tin. Mix the lemon juice, paprika and salt together and rub all over the bird. Set aside to marinate at room temperature for 1 hour. Preheat the oven to 220°C/Gas 7.

For the stuffing, put the cashew nuts in a mini food processor with the hot water and blend to a coarse paste. Add the spices, salt and yogurt and blend to combine. Divide the mixture between two bowls and mix one batch with the pork mince.

To stuff the chicken, turn it so the legs and cavity are facing you. Find the loose flap of skin above the cavity that covers the breast and gently work your hands between the skin and the flesh to loosen the skin, being careful not to make any holes. Gently push the plain nut stuffing (without the pork) under the skin, massaging it down towards the neck so that it completely covers both sides of the breast. Spoon the pork and nut stuffing into the cavity of the bird. Rub the softened butter all over the chicken and spoon over some of the marinade juices.

Cover the chicken loosely with foil, put it in the oven and immediately lower the temperature to 180°C/Gas 4. Roast for 45 minutes then remove the foil, baste the chicken with the juices and roast for a further 30–45 minutes or until the chicken is cooked through (to check, pierce the thickest part of the thigh with a fork and make sure the juices are clear. If you have a probe thermometer, plunge it into the thickest part of the bird and make sure it reads 75°C, then check the temperature inside the cavity too).

Transfer to a board or platter and leave to rest in a warm place, loosely covered in foil, for 15 minutes while you make the gravy.

To make the gravy, pour off most of the fat from the roasting tin, leaving behind the juices. Place over a medium heat and whisk in the flour. Cook for a minute or two then gradually whisk in the stock, scraping up the browned bits from the bottom of the tin. Bring to a boil and bubble over a gentle heat for 10 minutes, or until reduced to a good gravy consistency (if you like a thinner gravy you may want to add more stock). Pour in any juices that have collected under the chicken and simmer for a further minute or two. Check for seasoning then pour through a sieve into a warm gravy jug.

BUTTER CHICKEN

In Australia butter chicken is as ubiquitous as chicken tikka masala is in the UK. I make the comparison with reason because they're virtually the same dish. This does lead me to wonder whether all the stories about how chicken tikka masala was invented in the UK are true. The most common one of these is that it was a way Indian restaurants had of refreshing chicken cooked in the tandoor and not sold, i.e. by putting it in a spicy tomato sauce and reheating it. In fact, the practice of marinating chicken in spiced yogurt and cooking it in the intense dry heat of a tandoor, then adding a delicious sauce of slow-cooked garlic and ginger with chilli, coriander, cinnamon, tomato, cream and a paste of cashew and pumpkin seeds, is an Amritsar classic. *Recipe photograph overleaf*

SERVES 4-6

4 large chicken breasts, skinned, each cut into 2 or 3 pieces at an angle

For the first marinade
Juice of 2 limes
1 tsp Kashmiri chilli powder
1 tsp salt

For the second marinade
50g natural yogurt
50g double cream
20g/4 cloves garlic, roughly chopped
25g/5cm ginger, roughly chopped
1 tsp *Garam masala* (page 303)
1 tsp turmeric
¾ tsp ground cumin
½ tsp beetroot powder (for colour; optional)

For the sauce
50g ghee
25g/5 cloves garlic, finely crushed
25g/5cm ginger, finely grated
400g tomato passata
½ tsp Kashmiri chilli powder
½ tsp ground coriander
½ tsp ground cumin
½ tsp ground cinnamon
½ tsp *Garam masala* (page 303)
1 tsp desiccated coconut
1½ tsp salt
200ml water
25g cashew nuts
25g pumpkin seeds
2 tbsp boiling water
1 tbsp dried fenugreek leaves
½ tsp caster sugar
45ml double cream

To finish
Pinch of *Chat masala* (page 303)
Handful of coriander leaves, roughly chopped
15g/3cm ginger, finely shredded

For the first marinade, mix the lime juice, chilli powder and salt together in a large bowl. Add the chicken pieces to the marinade, then cover and transfer to the fridge to marinate for 1 hour.

For the second marinade, put all the ingredients apart from the chat masala into a mini food processor. Blend until smooth, then add this to the marinated chicken and stir well to coat. Cover and transfer to the fridge to marinate for 4 hours.

Preheat the oven to 240°C/Gas 9 (or 220°C if your oven doesn't go that high). Thread the chicken on to lightly oiled metal skewers (you can put more than one piece per skewer, but leave space between them) then suspend the skewers above a roasting tin. Alternatively place them on a wire rack over a roasting tin. Roast for 15–20 minutes, or until lightly charred in places but not completely cooked through, as you'll finish cooking them in the sauce.

For the sauce, while the chicken is cooking, heat the ghee in heavy-based saucepan or karahi over a medium heat. Add the garlic and ginger and fry for a minute, then stir in the tomato passata and bring to a simmer for 5 minutes. Add all the spices, coconut, salt and 100ml of the water and simmer for a further 10 minutes.

In a mini food processor, or using a pestle and mortar, blend the cashew nuts, pumpkin seeds and boiling water into a paste. Stir this into the sauce followed by the chicken pieces and another 100ml water.

Simmer for 10 minutes, or until the chicken is completely cooked through, then stir in the fenugreek leaves, sugar and cream and cook for a further 2 minutes. Sprinkle with chat masala, garnish with fresh coriander and ginger, and serve.

CHICKEN AND ROSEWATER BIRYANI

I've spent a considerable amount of time trying to perfect the making of a good biryani and the much easier pulao. Both are rice dishes with strong Persian influences, and when poorly made both are rather nastily stodgy. The rice in a biryani should be so dry and fluffy that when you throw a handful on the floor, all the grains should separate. The secret is to parboil the rice so that surface is soft and cooked but the centre is still hard, and also to make sure that the main ingredient, i.e. the chicken, mutton, seafood or vegetables, is intensely flavoured but not surrounded by too much 'gravy', which will make the rice soggy when the final cooking in a sealed pot takes place. I wrote this recipe from scratch so that the dish is as easy as possible to make. It does look like a lot of instructions but once you've made it and it works, it's a pleasure to cook, a bit like making a paella. Success gives you considerable elation. This is also successful with best end of neck lamb chops.

SERVES 6-8

500g skinless, boneless
   chicken thighs, cut in half

For the marinade
250ml natural yogurt
6 cloves (30g) garlic,
   finely crushed
6cm (30g) piece ginger,
   finely grated
3 green chillies, finely
   chopped, with seeds
1 tsp Kashmiri chilli powder
1 tsp ground coriander
½ tsp turmeric

For the crisp fried onions
300ml vegetable oil
3 medium onions, thinly sliced
10 whole cloves
6cm piece of cinnamon stick
5 green cardamom pods,
   bruised with a rolling pin
2 Indian bay leaves
1 tsp cumin seeds
2 medium tomatoes, chopped
1 tsp salt

For the rice
600g basmati rice, soaked
   in cold water for 1 hour
1 tsp salt per litre of
   cooking water

To assemble
100g ghee
Pinch of saffron soaked
   in 4 tbsp warm milk
   for 15 minutes
2 tsp rosewater
20g cashew nuts and 20g
   pistachios, dry-roasted
   in a hot pan until golden

To serve
Raita (page 304)

Combine all the marinade ingredients, add the chicken pieces, toss to coat well then set aside to marinate for an hour.

For the crisp fried onions, heat the vegetable oil in a sturdy pan or karahi over a medium heat until hot but not smoking. Add the onions and fry for 10–15 minutes or until deep golden brown. Remove with a slotted spoon and drain on kitchen paper. Set aside. Pour off all but about 3 tablespoons of the oil from the pan. (You can pour the oil off into a jug and set aside for another use.)

Add the whole spices to the pan and fry for 1 minute. Add the chicken and its marinade, bring to a simmer, then stir in the tomatoes and salt. Simmer over a medium heat for 20 minutes until the chicken is cooked through and the sauce is clinging to the chicken (add a splash of water to the pan if it catches on the bottom). It's important that the sauce is almost dry by this stage and just coating the chicken. Keep it warm on a low heat while you cook the rice.

Drain the soaked rice and tip into a large pan of boiling salted (at a rate of 1 tsp per litre of water) water for 5–7 minutes, until the rice is just tender but still firm, then drain well. Test that the rice is cooked by squeezing a grain between your fingers – it should be soft and break up at the edges, but stay firm in the middle.

Assemble the biryani straight away while the rice is still hot – you are aiming for 5 layers: rice, chicken, rice, chicken, rice. First pour about 3 tablespoons of water and half the ghee into a deep, heavy-based cooking pot or casserole, then spoon in a third of the rice. Sprinkle over about a third of the saffron milk and rosewater, then spread with half the chicken mixture and a third of the fried onions. Add another third of the rice and repeat as above, using the rest of the chicken. Top with the remaining rice and splash with the remaining saffron milk and rosewater. Set the remaining fried onions aside for now. Drizzle the remaining ghee around the edges of the rice so it drips down the inside of the pan.

Cover with a well-fitting lid. Put over a high heat to get the ghee hot and some steam going – lift up the lid to check. As soon as you see steam rising, turn down to a very low heat and cook for 30 minutes.

Spoon out on to a large serving platter and scatter with the rest of the crisp onions and toasted cashews and pistachios. Serve with raita.

CHETTINAD CHICKEN

When I heard that the Taj Gateway hotel in Madurai had employed a local housewife to cook some of the region's dishes, I knew they were on to something. Wherever you go in India, what people love above all is home cooking. I was lucky enough to watch Mrs Samundeswary cook her Chettinad chicken there. The dish is very peppery, but you know you're experiencing real country cooking. It also has one of those ingredients that is transformational but quite hard to get hold of. It's the lichen off a tree, known as dagarful, kalpasi or stone flower, with a flavour like cinnamon. You can find it online, but if it proves elusive, just add more cinnamon.

SERVES 4

RECIPE NOTE
If using dagarful, sort through it and remove and discard any pieces of bark first.

For the spice blend
1 tbsp fennel seeds
1 tbsp cumin seeds
1 tbsp coriander seeds
1 tbsp black peppercorns
1 tbsp Kashmiri chilli powder

For the chicken
50ml vegetable oil
1 tsp fennel seeds
5cm piece cinnamon bark
1 tbsp very roughly chopped dagarful or an extra 3cm piece cinnamon stick

150g shallots, diced
Handful of curry leaves
700g skinless boneless chicken thighs, cut into 5cm pieces
20g/4 cloves garlic, finely crushed
20g/4cm ginger, finely grated
1 tsp sugar
1 tsp salt
100ml water
Boiled basmati rice (page 313), to serve

For the spice blend, put the spices in a spice grinder and process to a powder.

For the chicken, heat the oil in a sturdy frying pan or karahi over a medium heat, add the fennel, cinnamon and dagarful and fry for 1 minute. Add the shallots and curry leaves and fry for 10 minutes until the shallots are softened and golden. Add the chicken and stir around for 1-2 minutes, then stir in the garlic, ginger, sugar, salt and all of the spice blend, and fry for 2 minutes. Add the water, and cook for about 10–15 minutes, stirring often and adding more splashes of water if needed to stop it sticking to the pan, until the chicken is cooked through and the sauce thick and reduced and clinging to the chicken. Serve with boiled rice.

CHICKEN SKEWERS WITH CARDAMOM

This recipe was created by the head chef of the Spice Village at Thekkady in Kerala. When I first tasted this I was extremely excited because I realized how simple the recipe was, and it's essential for a book like this to have a fair smattering of recipes you can knock up in, dare I say it, 15 minutes, give or take 3 hours' marinating. What I particularly like about it, apart from the simplicity, is that it very much features the flavour of one spice, cardamom; the sprinkling of chat masala at the end is merely an exotic finishing touch. In Australia you can buy jars of cardamom seeds; you can't get them in Britain. Anybody take the hint?

SERVES 4-6

RECIPE NOTE
You need skewers for this dish; if using bamboo or wooden skewers, soak in water for an hour or so first.

750g skinless, boneless chicken thighs, cut into 4cm pieces
Juice of 1 lime
2 fresh red chillies, finely chopped, with or without seeds according to preference
75g ginger, grated
3 tbsp thick Greek-style yogurt
2 tbsp double cream
2 tbsp coconut cream

¾ tsp salt
½ tsp coarsely ground black pepper
½ tsp ground cardamom (seeds from about 15 green pods)
2 tbsp vegetable oil
Pinch of *Chat masala* (optional; page 303)
Rick's everyday pilau rice (page 307), to serve

Mix the chicken, lime juice, chillies and ginger together in a bowl and marinate for 15 minutes.

In another bowl mix together the yogurt, cream and coconut cream, then stir in the salt, black pepper and cardamom. Mix with the chicken and marinate in the fridge for a further 2–3 hours.

Preheat the grill to high, or heat a sturdy griddle or frying pan over a high heat (or light a barbecue). Thread the chicken on to skewers, brush with oil and cook for 3–4 minutes on each side, until charred in places and cooked through. Sprinkle with chat masala, if using, and serve with rice.

DUCK ROAST
Tharavu roast

This is a typical Syrian Christian Keralan dish. You rub the duck with a blend of spices, roast it in lots of ghee, make a delicious masala of onions and more spices, carve the duck up and pop it in the masala to heat through before serving.

SERVES 4-6

RECIPE NOTE
This uses the duck giblets to make a stock. If you can't get a duck with giblets, you can use 400ml chicken stock instead and infuse it with the spices.

For the spice mix
6 cloves
6 green cardamom pods
4cm piece of cinnamon stick
1 tsp black peppercorns
1 tsp black mustard seeds
1 tbsp Kashmiri chilli powder
1 tsp turmeric
5 tbsp water

For the duck
1 x 2kg duck, with giblets
1 tsp salt
50g ghee

For the stock
1 large onion, sliced
50g/10 cloves garlic, finely chopped
50g ginger, finely chopped
Giblets from the duck
400ml water (or chicken stock if not using giblets)

For the masala
50ml vegetable oil
2 large onions, sliced
½ tsp salt
Chipped potatoes roasted in ghee, to serve

For the spice mix, grind the cloves, cardamoms, cinnamon stick, peppercorns and mustard seeds into a fine powder. Mix with the chilli powder, turmeric and water.

For the duck, preheat the oven to 160°C/Gas 3. Remove the giblets from the duck and reserve. Season the cavity with about a quarter of the spice mix, then rub the outside with the salt and place in a roasting tin. Cover tightly with foil and roast for 1 hour. Increase the oven temperature to 220°C/Gas 7. Uncover the duck and spoon over the ghee. Roast for 20–30 minutes or until the skin is crisp and browned and the duck is cooked through. Rest for 10 minutes, then carve.

While the duck is roasting, make the stock. Put the onion, garlic and ginger into a large pan with another quarter of the spice mix. Add the reserved giblets and water (or chicken stock). Bring to the boil, then simmer for 30 minutes. Strain.

For the masala, heat the oil in a heavy-based saucepan or karahi over a medium heat and fry the onions for 10 minutes until softened and browned. Lower the heat, stir in the remaining spice mix and the salt, and fry for 2–3 minutes. Add the strained stock to the pan, bring to the boil, then lower the heat and simmer for 2–3 minutes to allow the flavours to infuse. Add the pieces of carved duck and heat through. Serve with chips.

GOSHT

...deep and dark meat curries, kormas, pulaos and biryanis

David Pritchard, the director I've worked with for all my TV career, thinks I should start a little farm in Cornwall called Goats by the Sea on the strength of how successful this book on curries is going to be. Because there is a problem, a dichotomy if you like – most people in Britain find curries made with goat meat on the bone a little off-putting, whereas Indians massively prefer what they call mutton curry, which is in fact curry of young goat, to lamb. Indians use the English language to suit themselves, not to suit us, and they use the word mutton to describe goat meat. They say our lamb is too fatty for a good curry. I must say, after being in India for a while, I can see what they mean. The unctuousness of Indian mutton curries comes from long, slow cooking of meat and all the connective tissues – they adore lean meat. I've come to enjoy their style of curry but I still really love the richness of lamb in a curry too. So I've adapted all the recipes for cooking lamb. Saying that, it's much easier to get goat these days because there are several farms producing goat meat for the table, as opposed to having goat meat as a byproduct of the milk. And watch this space for Goats by the Sea ...

While I well understand the enthusiasm for mutton on the bone, finding good beef in India is difficult simply because there is so little production of it, thanks to the cow being held as sacred. Only in areas with high Christian populations do you find beef dishes regularly on the menu, and because cattle are generally slaughtered for consumption the same day you buy the meat, the beef is extraordinarily tough, so a recipe like the Goan beef vindaloo on page 266 requires significant marination of the meat in vinegar and spices before a long, slow cooking.

Pork is little found outside Kerala and Goa. Muslims don't eat it; many Hindus are vegetarians, and those who do eat meat don't care for pork. But I think the pork dishes of the Christian communities in Goa and Kerala are a triumph of fragrance and use of spice balanced with a delicate sourness from vinegar, or tamarind, as in my recipe for pork and green chillies (page 274).

Shortly after I returned from filming there was a furore in Britain over the fraudulent inclusion of horsemeat in beef mince. I doubt this could ever happen in India, or certainly not in Kerala, because it's customary when you've slaughtered an ox to display its head at the front of your shop as proof of what the customer is buying. The same happens with mutton. You will normally get the head and forefeet as an indication of quality and freshness. I recall years ago in a butcher's in St Merryn near Padstow seeing a calf's head on the slab and hearing a lady behind me saying, 'I don't think we need to see that in here.' There is a refreshing honesty about traceability in India.

SHAMI KEBABS

One of the people helping me with this book, Roopa Gulati, introduced me to the Amaya restaurant in Knightsbridge, and there I discovered the pleasures of shami kebabs. I was also introduced to the story behind kebabs like them: that the dish was invented by a highly skilled chef for a toothless Nawab of Lucknow. The Nawab was so fat from overindulgence that he couldn't get on a horse, and his teeth were all gone, presumably for the same reason. So a kebab was made so fine that it required no teeth to eat it. When I hear stories like that I'm inclined to think, 'If you believe that, you'll believe anything.' But then again, it's a nice story, and so are the kebabs – silky smooth and stuffed with just a little finely chopped onion, mint and green chilli.
Recipe photograph overleaf

**MAKES
16–20 KEBABS**

90g chana dal (Bengal gram or split yellow peas), soaked in cold water for about an hour
2 medium onions, roughly chopped
40g/8 cloves garlic, peeled
60g ginger, roughly chopped
2 tbsp water
2 tbsp ghee or vegetable oil
500g lamb mince
1 tsp salt
3 fresh green chillies, roughly chopped, with seeds
Handful of coriander leaves, chopped
1 tsp *Garam masala* (page 303)
½ tsp Kashmiri chilli powder
½ tsp black cumin (shahi zeera) or regular cumin seeds
Juice of 1 lime
1 free-range egg, lightly beaten
About 2 tbsp plain flour, to bind
Vegetable oil, for shallow-frying

For the filling
1 medium red onion, finely chopped
Juice of 1 lime
1 fresh green chilli, finely chopped, without seeds
Handful of mint leaves, finely shredded
¼ tsp sugar
¼ tsp salt

To serve
Lime wedges, red onion rings and *Green chutney* (page 303)

Drain the split peas and put them aside. Put the onions, garlic, ginger and water in a mini food processor and blend to a paste.

Heat the ghee or oil in a heavy-based saucepan over a medium heat, add the onion paste and cook for 10 minutes. Stir in the lamb mince and split peas, pour over enough water to just cover the meat (about 400ml), add ½ teaspoon salt, partially cover with a lid and bring to a simmer. Cook for about 20 minutes, until most of the liquid has evaporated. Remove the lid and cook for a further 5–10 minutes, until the meat is just starting to brown and catch on the bottom. It's important that any excess moisture has evaporated. Transfer to a plate and leave to cool for about 15 minutes, then tip into a food processor and blend to a smooth paste.

Add the green chillies, coriander, garam masala, chilli powder, cumin, the remaining salt and the lime juice to the lamb mixture and blend again, then gradually add enough of the egg to bind the mixture without making it too wet. Transfer to a bowl and stir in the flour to create a mixture you can shape.

In a separate bowl, mix together all the filling ingredients. Drain off any liquid just before assembling.

To shape the kebabs, wet your hands and divide the mixture into about 16–20 portions. (If you find the mixture is still a little too wet to shape into patties, then add another tablespoon of flour.) Shape one portion into a patty about 4cm in diameter and ½ cm thick. Put ¾ teaspoon of the red onion and mint filling in the middle of the patty, and draw the edges around and over it to encase the filling and form a rough ball. Then flatten it into a 5mm-thick patty. Place on a tray, repeat with the remaining mixture, then chill in the fridge for an hour before cooking.

To fry the kebabs, heat a few tablespoons of oil in a heavy-based frying pan over a medium heat. Fry the patties in batches for 2–3 minutes on each side until golden brown and cooked through.

Sprinkle with a little extra salt, and serve warm with lime wedges, red onion rings and green chutney on the side.

LAMB CUTLETS SPICED WITH FENNEL
Shahi chaap amber

Lunching at Sanjiv Bali's restaurant in the Amber Fort just outside Jaipur turned out to be a showcase of classic Rajasthani cuisine. In addition to the jungli maas curry on page 260, he also produced a safed maas, which is a white mutton curry (page 265) and this popular mutton chop recipe, which we made with lamb cutlets, first simmered in aromatic milk before being given a light spice batter and fried. It is highly tempting to pick one up and nibble at it before anyone else has had a chance.

SERVES 4–6

For the lamb
12 green cardamom pods,
   lightly bruised with
   a rolling pin
12 cloves
8cm piece of cinnamon stick
2 tsp fennel seeds
2 Indian bay leaves
1½ tsp black peppercorns
1 tsp ground ginger
1.5 litres whole milk
500ml water
1kg lamb cutlets
   (from a rack of lamb)
75ml vegetable oil

For the batter
250g plain flour
2 tsp cornflour
2 tsp ground black pepper
2 tsp toasted ground
   fennel seeds
1 tsp ground ginger
1 tsp ground cardamom
   (seeds from 30 green pods)
1 tsp salt
3 green chillies, finely
   chopped, with seeds
2 egg whites
Pinch of *Chat masala*
   (page 303), to finish

Put the cardamom pods, cloves, cinnamon stick, fennel seeds, bay leaves, black peppercorns and ginger into a deep, sturdy pan and add the milk and water. Simmer gently for 10 minutes. Add the lamb cutlets and simmer very gently for 10 minutes. Leave to cool in the liquid (the lamb should still be pink in the middle at this stage).

Make the batter by sifting together the flour and cornflour, then stir in the black pepper, fennel, ginger, cardamom and salt, followed by the chillies. Lightly beat the egg whites until just frothy then whisk into the dry ingredients with enough of the cool milky stock to make a thin batter the consistency of single cream. Add the cooled cutlets to the batter and turn to coat evenly.

Heat the vegetable oil in a large frying pan over a medium heat. Take a few cutlets from the batter, add to the pan (don't overcrowd it) and fry for 2–3 minutes on each side until golden brown. Keep these warm while you cook the rest. Sprinkle with chat masala, and serve hot.

RED CHILLI LAMB
Lal maas

The distinguishing feature of this dish is the amount of red chillies in it. It's a classic Rajasthani dish made with the local red chillies called Mathania, which are a lot hotter than the Kashmiri chillies I've specified. In either case it's the deep-red colour that really matters. If you can get hold of Mathanias, watch out! I was rather amused when we visited the hunting lodge of the Singh family, whose castle we were staying at, because David Pritchard, the director, was complaining that we were filming with too many Rajputs, i.e. Rajasthani royalty. But I couldn't help feeling it would make wonderful pictures – the lodge, the fabulous lamb curry being cooked outside, the lake, the lilies, the water chestnuts…

SERVES 4-6

4 tsp coriander seeds
3 black cardamom pods,
    seeds only
25 dried Kashmiri chillies,
    stalks snipped off
300ml thick Greek-style yogurt
3 Indian bay leaves
¾ tsp turmeric

1kg shoulder of lamb, on the bone,
    cut into 3cm-thick slices (ask
    your butcher to do this for you)
100g ghee
3 medium onions, sliced
50g/10 cloves garlic,
    finely crushed
1 tsp salt

Grind the coriander, cardamom seeds and chillies to a coarse powder in a spice grinder (or pestle and mortar). Mix all but 1 teaspoon with the yogurt, bay leaves and turmeric in a large bowl. Add the lamb and mix to coat. Leave for 30 minutes.

Heat the ghee in a heavy-based saucepan or karahi over a medium heat and fry the onions and garlic for 10–15 minutes until golden. Add the lamb and its yogurt marinade and fry over a medium heat for about 20 minutes, until any moisture evaporates and lamb turns a deep brown – add a splash of water if the lamb starts to catch on the bottom of the pan.

Pour over enough water to barely cover the meat and stir in the salt, cover with a tight-fitting lid and cook very gently for about an hour, until the lamb is tender and the sauce thickened. Sprinkle with the remaining teaspoon of spices and serve.

LAMB AND YOGURT CURRY WITH GREEN CHILLIES AND SOUR PLUMS
Rezala

Rezala is a Muslim speciality popular in Bangladesh and Bengal, and also famous with the Muslim community in Bhopal. Its great claim to fame is how very easy it is to make, but paradoxically for us it includes a type of tiny sour plum called alu Bukhara which is not widely available. Nevertheless, I think a sour fruit element is satisfying in this dish; you can get alu Bukhara from Asian supermarkets, but sour cherries, which you can get anywhere, would be as good, or you could even use fresh sloes. *Recipe photograph overleaf*

SERVES 4

100g ghee
500g boneless leg of lamb,
    cut into 3cm cubes
175g green chillies, cut
    lengthwise, without seeds
225ml thick Greek-style yogurt
120g fresh coriander, chopped
1 large onion, very finely sliced

60g ginger, finely chopped
15g/3 cloves garlic, crushed
10 dried sour plums
    (alu Bukhara) or 15
    dried sour cherries
1 tsp toasted ground
    cumin seeds
½ tsp salt

Melt the ghee in a sturdy pan over a medium heat, then add all the remaining ingredients (you're not aiming to brown the meat in this dish). Cover tightly with foil and a well-fitting lid, making sure the steam can't escape. Cook over a low heat for an hour, or until the meat is tender. (You can also cook it in the oven preheated to 160°C/Gas 3 for about an hour.) Serve.

LAMB DOPIAZA

I found this speciality of Bengal in *The Calcutta Cook Book*. I was struck by its simplicity. All the ingredients go into a pot and are simply simmered together until they're cooked. Would this work, I wondered? It did. It was a total triumph, and sort of makes you wonder why you bother roasting, frying, adding bits here and there. The main author of the book was Minakshie Das Gupta; the recipe was contributed by Mrs Tara Sinha, who got it from Mrs Sita Pasricha. Where would we be without the contributions to cookery books of good, trustworthy, female home cooks?

SERVES 4

500g lamb shoulder,
  cut into 4cm pieces
1kg onions, cut into quarters
30g/6 cloves garlic,
  finely chopped
15g/3cm ginger, finely sliced
500g natural yogurt
4 tsp coriander seeds
1 tsp turmeric

2 tsp cumin seeds
1 tsp cloves
10cm piece of cinnamon stick
10 dried Kashmiri chillies
1 tsp black peppercorns
6 green cardamom pods, bruised
6 tbsp ghee or butter
1½ tbsp salt
250ml water

Tip all the ingredients into a deep pan, mix together, cover with a tight-fitting lid and bring gently to a boil. Simmer over a low heat for 2 hours, until almost all the liquid has been absorbed and the lamb is tender. Serve.

LAMB AND SWEET POTATO CURRY IN ONION MASALA
Dabi arvi ka salan

This is a very nice lamb and sweet potato curry, and being a Lucknow dish it's not particularly hot with chilli, but plays more on the warming aromas of fragrant spices. Being a Lucknow dish it also has a bit of a theatrical case of mistaken identity, just to keep the courtiers in the Nawab's palace guessing. Originally it was made with taro root as well as lamb, which when fried looks like a little like meat so that nobody knew what they were eating. Making taro look like meat is a long process and nobody's going to do it unless they've got the sort of kitchen brigade they would have had then. I've just put sweet potato in instead, which is lovely. I have to confess, too, that I've cut down the 25-ingredient Lucknow masala to my standard garam masala with some ground fennel seeds and allspice. You could add some dried, ground rose petals if you had them.

SERVES 4–6

250g ghee
1 large onion, sliced
450g sweet potato,
    cut into 3–4cm chunks
750g boneless lamb shoulder,
    cut into 4cm pieces
75g ginger, finely grated
35g/7 cloves garlic,
    finely chopped
1 tsp Kashmiri chilli powder

1 tbsp *Garam masala*
    (page 303)
1 tsp white pepper
1 tsp toasted ground
    fennel seeds
1 tsp ground allspice
2 tsp salt
100ml thick Greek-style yogurt
Handful of chopped
    coriander, to finish

Heat the ghee in a large, sturdy pan over a medium-high heat and fry the onion for 10 minutes until softened and browned. Remove with a slotted spoon, leaving behind excess ghee, and purée in a mini food processor with a splash of water. Set aside.

Add the sweet potato to the same pan and fry for 5 minutes until golden brown. Remove with a slotted spoon and drain on kitchen paper. Next, brown the lamb in the pan, then add the ginger and garlic and fry for 3–4 minutes until aromatic. Add the onion purée, chilli powder, half the garam masala, the white pepper, fennel, allspice and salt, and cook for a minute. Stir in the yogurt and cook for 3–4 minutes to reduce slightly, then add enough water to cover the lamb and bring to a simmer. Cover and simmer for 1 hour, until the meat is tender, then add the sweet potato and enough water for a thick broth-like consistency. Simmer, uncovered, for 10–15 minutes. Stir in the remaining garam masala, sprinkle with coriander and serve.

LAMB PULAO
Idris yakhni pulao

I know this is only an academic point, but I'm blowed if I can see how this pulao isn't a biryani. As I see it, the main difference between a biryani and pulao is that in a biryani the rice is precooked and in a pulao it isn't – yet the rice in this pulao is precooked. And a certain amount of layering of rice and lamb takes place. But who am I to say? It's lovely, and don't be put off by the large amount of rice in it relative to the lamb and masala – biryanis and pulaos are all about the rice. When we filmed the making of this in Lucknow at the pulao joint called Idris, I realized halfway through that my recipe would have to be a reconstruction. There were so many confusing stages to it, perhaps because Idris's family was so large, and so many of his relatives had a part to play in putting together their famous pulaos, of which they sell over three hundred a day. But they were great people. After we'd filmed it we all sat in their family home round the corner, eating pulao and drinking Coke.

Recipe photograph overleaf

SERVES 8–10

50g ghee or 50ml vegetable oil
6 cloves
4 green cardamom pods, lightly
  bruised with a rolling pin
5cm piece of cinnamon stick
1 medium onion, sliced
25g/5 cloves garlic,
  finely crushed
25g/5cm ginger, finely grated
1½ tsp Kashmiri chilli powder
1 tsp ground cumin
½ tsp ground cardamom
  (or seeds from 15 pods)
1 tsp sugar
2 tsp salt
1kg boneless lamb shoulder,
  cut into large pieces
  roughly 2cm thick and
  measuring 5cm x 3cm
600ml water
300ml double cream

For the saffron-infused milk
300ml milk
Big pinch of saffron
1 tbsp rosewater
12 drops screwpine essence
  or 1 tbsp screwpine water
  (optional)

For the rice
800g basmati rice, soaked
  in cold water for 1 hour
6 green cardamom pods, lightly
  bruised with a rolling pin
6 cloves

In a large casserole dish or karahi, heat the ghee or oil over a medium heat and add the cloves, cardamom pods and cinnamon stick, fry for 30 seconds to 1 minute until fragrant, then add the onion and fry for 10 minutes until softened and golden. Add the garlic and ginger, fry for a minute, then add the chilli powder, ground cumin, ground cardamom, sugar and salt and fry for 30 seconds.

Add all the lamb and stir to mix, then pour in the water. Bring to a simmer, turn the heat to low, partly cover with a lid and cook very gently for 45 minutes to 1 hour until the lamb is tender and the liquid is reduced to about 75ml. Remove from the heat and stir in the cream.

For the saffron-infused milk, gently heat the milk until lukewarm then take off the heat, add the saffron, rosewater, and screwpine if using, and leave to infuse while you cook the rice.

For the rice, bring a large pan with 4 litres of water and 4 teaspoons of salt to a rolling boil over a high heat. Add the soaked, drained basmati rice, cardamom pods and cloves and bring back to the boil. As soon as it starts to boil, remove a few grains of rice and check they are ready: rub a grain between your fingers – the outer part should be soft and break up but the centre should still be firm and hold its shape. If it's ready, drain straight away, otherwise cook further, checking for doneness every minute.

Assemble the pulao straight away while the rice is still hot. Spoon half the rice on top of the lamb then spoon over the saffron-infused milk. Top with the rest of the rice. Cover with a well-fitting lid and cook over a medium heat for 30 minutes. Just before serving, take a ladle and scoop some of the lamb and sauce from the bottom of the pan and fold gently through the layers of rice – the aim is not to mix everything together but to create a pleasing contrast between lamb and white and yellow rice.

LAMB KORMA
Shahi korma

This dish is rich and uses a large amount of ghee – which is typical of Rajasthan. The flavour of ghee is an important part of a korma. Thakur Man Singh gave me this korma recipe when I visited him at his home, Castle Kanota, just outside Jaipur. It was one that his grandfather Thakur Amar Singh had collected; in all he produced sixty volumes of recipes as he travelled India and then Europe with the Jodhpur Lancers during the First World War. He was able to purchase the castle and another large home in Jaipur itself with his earnings from the British Army. Perhaps this is why he says in one of his books, 'Well-cooked English food is just as much to my taste as the Indian. I might say that if there is Indian food and one has to eat with knives and forks then there is no fun. In the same way if there is English food and one has to eat it without knives and forks then it loses the enjoyment.' I must say I still haven't mastered the art of eating this mild but aromatic korma with my fingers.

SERVES 4–6

2 medium onions,
  roughly chopped
100g ghee
75g ginger, shredded
1 tsp salt
750g boneless leg of lamb,
  cut into 3cm chunks
2 tbsp roughly chopped
  dried coconut strips
  (available in Indian shops)
  or desiccated coconut

50g almonds, blanched
  and thinly sliced
1½ tsp *Garam masala*
  (page 303)

To serve
Indian breads (page 306)

Preheat the oven to 150°C/Gas 2. Tip the onions into a mini food processor and blend to a paste, adding a splash of water if needed.

Heat the ghee in a sturdy ovenproof pan over a medium heat and fry the onion for 10 minutes until golden. Add the ginger and salt and cook for a further 2 minutes, then add the lamb and fry, stirring occasionally and adding a splash of water if it starts to catch, for 15–20 minutes. Stir in about 50ml water and scrape any browned bits off the bottom of the pan, then add the coconut, almonds and garam masala.

Cover the pan and transfer to the oven to cook for 30 minutes, or until the lamb is tender and the masala thickened and quite dry. Serve with breads.

FRIED MINCED LAMB WITH GARLIC, GREEN CHILLI AND CORIANDER
Keema kaleji

This recipe comes from the Pal dhaba in the centre of Amristar, just by the Hathi (Elephant) Gate. The dhaba has distinctive white and green tiled walls and specializes in very tasty parathas. There's nothing quite like a dhaba anywhere outside of India and Pakistan. Part diner, part truck stop, part bustling roadside café, a dhaba is a dhaba. There is one element in the dish that I think absolutely makes it: lamb's liver. The recipe calls for 200g; you can leave it out or just try putting in 50g or 80g. This, rolled up in a flaky flatbread and with a glass or two of Kingfisher beer, would be hard to beat. *Recipe photograph overleaf*

SERVES 4

5 tbsp vegetable oil
1 tsp cumin seeds
1 tsp chilli flakes
3 large onions, diced
500g lamb mince
100ml thick Greek-style yogurt
50g ginger, finely grated
40g/8 cloves garlic, finely chopped
1 tsp turmeric
4 fresh green chillies, roughly chopped, without seeds

1 tsp salt
200g lamb's liver, membrane removed, cut into 3cm pieces
¾ tsp toasted ground cumin seeds
Juice of 1 lime
Handful of fresh coriander, chopped

To serve
Parathas (page 306)

Heat 3 tablespoons of the vegetable oil in a heavy-based saucepan or karahi set over a medium heat and add the cumin and chilli flakes. Fry for 30 seconds until fragrant, then add the onions and fry for 10–15 minutes until softened and golden brown.

Combine the mince with the yogurt, ginger, garlic and turmeric and mix well, then add to the pan of onions and fry for 10 minutes, or until browned. Add the green chillies, salt and enough water to cover the mince. Simmer, uncovered, for about 10–15 minutes, until the mince is cooked and the sauce reduced and thickened.

Meanwhile, heat the remaining 2 tablespoons of oil in a frying pan over a medium-high heat. Add the lamb's liver and fry for 1–2 minutes on each side, until browned on the outside but still pink and tender in the middle. Sprinkle over the cumin and lime juice, stir well and add to the cooked mince. Cook for another minute, then add the chopped coriander. Serve with parathas.

SHEPHERD'S PIE AS INSPIRED BY THE MADRAS CLUB

As I've mentioned elsewhere in this book, the memories of British Raj cooking are still alive in India, particularly in the British Raj Club in Chennai. This dish, not entirely the same recipe but my interpretation of it, is still on the menu there and is very popular.

SERVES 6

For the spiced mince filling
2 tbsp vegetable oil
400g onions, thinly sliced
25g/5 cloves garlic,
    finely chopped
20g/4cm ginger, finely grated
900g minced lamb
1 tsp turmeric
1½ tsp Kashmiri chilli powder
2 tbsp *Garam masala* (page 303)

1 x 400g tin chopped tomatoes
600ml chicken stock or water
1½ tsp salt

For the potato topping
1.25kg floury potatoes,
    peeled and cut into chunks
½ tsp salt
50g butter
100ml milk

For the spiced mince, heat the oil in a thick-bottomed pan or karahi on a medium heat. Add the onions, garlic and ginger, and fry for 10 minutes until softened and golden brown. Add the minced lamb, turmeric, chilli powder and garam masala and fry for 2 minutes. Stir in the tomatoes and stock, season with the salt and simmer for 30 minutes until the mixture has thickened but is still moist. Transfer to a 1.75-litre ovenproof dish.

Preheat the oven to 200°C/Gas 6. For the potato topping, cook the potatoes in plenty of boiling, salted water for about 10 minutes or until completely tender. Drain well then tip back into the pan, place over a low heat, and add the salt, butter and enough of the milk to form a soft, spreadable mash.

Spoon the potato over the lamb. Place the dish on a baking tray in the oven and bake for 30–35 minutes until golden brown.

MR SINGH'S SLOW-COOKED LAMB CURRY WITH CLOVES AND CARDAMOM

I'm sure there are unpleasant Sikhs out there, it's just that I've never met one. They all seem to be immaculately turned out: smart clothes, sensible shoes, trim beards, tidy turbans and always a welcoming smile. About to fly from Delhi to Amritsar, I noticed the captain through the window, checking the engines. He was magnificent in navy blue, big moustache and gold braid, and I thought, he'll look after us. Mr Balwant Singh was no exception. Charming, full of great information about choosing the right cut of mutton for this curry, and then cooking a most immaculate example of it for us outside on a sunny day – well, it's always sunny in the Punjab apart from the monsoons. He took us to where his father had set up refugee camps on their family land and cooked this curry to give the displaced people a taste of home cooking. I've used lamb shoulder, with goat as an option; you could also use lamb neck fillet. *Recipe photograph overleaf*

SERVES 4-6

½ tsp cardamom seeds
 (from about 8 green pods)
4–6 cloves
3 medium onions
200g tomatoes
50g/10 cloves garlic
20g/4cm ginger
75ml vegetable oil or 75g ghee
100ml thick Greek-style yogurt

700g boneless lamb shoulder,
 trimmed of excess fat, cut into
 4cm pieces, or 1kg goat on the
 bone, cut into 7cm pieces
1 tsp salt
1 tsp *Garam masala* (page 303)
1 tsp Kashmiri chilli powder
1 tbsp single cream
Chapatis (page 306), to serve

Grind the cardamom and cloves into a powder; set aside. In stages, using a mini food processor and rinsing out in between, roughly chop the onions then blend to a purée with a little water; roughly chop then purée the tomatoes; roughly chop then blend the garlic and ginger with a tablespoon of water to a slack paste.

Heat the oil or ghee in a heavy-based casserole pan over a medium heat and gently fry the onion paste for 10–15 minutes until golden, then add the ginger and garlic and fry for 3 minutes. Stir in the yogurt, then add the meat and salt and cook over a low-medium heat for 20–30 minutes until browned. Stir in the garam masala and chilli powder, and after about 30 seconds pour over enough water to just cover the meat. Simmer, covered, for 40 minutes.

Stir the cream and puréed tomatoes into the lamb, followed by the cardamom and clove mix. To seal the pan, first cover with foil, then a lid. Cook over the lowest heat for 30–40 minutes until the lamb is tender. Serve with chapatis.

COCHIN FIRST-CLASS RAILWAY MUTTON CURRY

Though described as a mutton curry, this is in fact made with lamb shanks. One of chef Ajeeth Janardhanan's signature dishes of the Brunton Boatyard Hotel in Fort Cochin, it is described as a secret recipe, but I can't see that I've left anything out. On the menu it says, 'The story goes that an English army officer, while travelling in a train, became ravenously hungry. He followed his nose to the pantry car, where a spicy mutton curry was simmering. He was offered a taste, whereupon he burnt his tongue because of the spices. The helpful cook reduced the pungency with some coconut milk and served it up. From that day on, this has become a staple on all first-class compartments of the train.' *Recipe photograph overleaf*

SERVES 6

RECIPE NOTE
The lamb needs marinating overnight.

For the marinade
15g/3cm ginger, finely grated
15g/3 cloves garlic, finely crushed
2 tbsp thick Greek-style yogurt
¼ tsp turmeric
6 lamb shanks

For the curry
100g cashew nuts
300g tomatoes
100ml vegetable oil
2 x 4cm pieces of cinnamon stick
4 cloves
7 green cardamom pods, lightly bruised with a rolling pin
¼ tsp ground mace
1 large onion, diced
1 tsp salt
100ml water
1 tbsp ground coriander
1 tbsp Kashmiri chilli powder
1 tsp turmeric
2 tsp *Garam masala* (page 303)
15g/3cm ginger, finely grated
15g/3 cloves garlic, finely crushed
2 Indian bay leaves
100ml coconut milk

For the marinade, combine the ginger, garlic, yogurt and turmeric, then add the lamb and mix together. Cover and leave to marinate in the fridge overnight.

For the curry, put the cashew nuts in a pan with the whole tomatoes and pour over just enough water to cover the tomatoes. Bring to a boil and simmer for 5 minutes, then leave to cool slightly. Transfer everything to a food processor and blend to a smooth purée. Set aside.

Preheat the oven to 150°C/Gas 2.

Heat the vegetable oil in a large, sturdy casserole over a medium-high heat, then add the cinnamon sticks, cloves, cardamom pods and mace. Fry for about 30 seconds until aromatic, then stir in the onion and salt and fry for 10 minutes until golden. Pour in the water, scraping any browned bits off the bottom of the pan, and let it bubble for a minute.

Stir in the coriander, chilli powder, turmeric, garam masala, ginger and garlic, and fry for 1–2 minutes until the spices are aromatic. Add the lamb and its marinade to the pan and fry for 10 minutes, stirring occasionally, until browned all over (add a splash of water if it starts to catch).

Pour in the cashew nut and tomato purée, bring to a simmer, then add the bay leaves. Cover the pan and transfer to the oven for 3 hours, or until the lamb is tender and the sauce rich and thickened. Check the liquid levels a couple of times during cooking, topping up with a little boiling water if needed.

Stir in the coconut milk, cover and leave to rest for 5 minutes, then serve.

NUTMEG

LAMB ROGAN JOSH

One of the greatest sources of new-dish information for me on my travels in India has been the hotel buffet. Much Indian cooking lends itself to being kept warm in chafing dishes and in a big hotel you might get as many as thirty or forty different curries. They're never going to be the best but you get a good idea of what you like and what you don't. So it was with this rogan josh from the Kenilworth Hotel in Calcutta. I liked it and asked the chef to cook it for me. Sadly we couldn't film in Kashmir, where the dish comes from, because of security problems. The dish comes originally from Persia where *rogan* means 'oil' and *josh* means 'hot'. In other words, this dish is cooked with intense heat. But *rogan* can also mean 'red', and above all this dish is red and satisfyingly spicy from Kashmiri chillies.

SERVES 4–6

40g ghee
5cm piece of cinnamon stick
3 dried Kashmiri chillies,
    torn into pieces
6 green cardamom pods, lightly
    bruised with a rolling pin
4 cloves
1 large onion, chopped
15g/3 cloves garlic,
    finely crushed
15g/3cm ginger, finely grated
2 tbsp Kashmiri chilli powder
1 tbsp ground coriander
1 tbsp ground cumin
2 tsp turmeric
¼ tsp ground mace

1 tsp *Garam masala* (page 303),
    plus 1 tsp extra to finish
1 tsp toasted ground fennel
    seeds, plus ¼ tsp extra
    to finish
4 tbsp tomato purée
750g boneless lamb shoulder,
    trimmed of excess fat,
    cut into 3cm cubes
1 tsp salt
300ml water
125g natural yogurt
50ml double cream
Handful of coriander
    leaves, roughly chopped,
    to finish

Put the ghee in a large, sturdy casserole over a medium heat. When hot, add the whole spices and fry for 1 minute, then add the onion and fry for 10 minutes until softened and golden. Stir in the garlic and ginger, fry for 1 minute, then add the ground spices (reserving the extra garam masala and ground fennel) and fry for 30 seconds.

Stir in the tomato purée, then add the lamb and salt and stir to make sure the lamb is well coated in the other ingredients. Pour in the water, bring to a simmer, then cover the pan, reduce the heat to low and simmer gently for 1 hour or until the lamb is tender. Stir in the yogurt and cream, then season with the extra garam masala and ground fennel. Scatter with the fresh coriander and serve.

LEG OF LAMB WITH RED CHILLIES AS COOKED BY HUNTERS IN RAJASTHAN
Jungli maas

Sanjiv Bali having a restaurant, 1135 AD, in the Amber Fort just outside Jaipur, would be a bit like someone persuading our government to let him open a restaurant in the middle of the Tower of London. The bureaucracy against such a thing happening was almost overwhelming, yet somehow he did it, and the fit out of the restaurant is so faithful to the rest of the fort that, but for the fact everything is new, you'd hardly notice. It's a tour de force of silver and gold, beautifully coloured mosaics, wonderful plastered floors and smoky mirrors. As he explained to me, the descendants of the craftsmen who would have been responsible for the interiors in the sixteenth century are still making the same gorgeous artefacts in Rajasthan today. The food does complete justice to all this; of the three recipes from a memorable lunch I had there, this is the simplest: only five ingredients, one of which is water. A classic dish made on hunting trips when a few ingredients, a pan and an open fire would have been all that was available. Traditionally this was made with game, but all game hunting, naturally including tigers, is now banned in India. It occurred to me at the time that this recipe could be well adapted to cooking a leg of lamb back home, and you could serve either British accompaniments like roast potatoes and spring greens or Indian like aloo gobi (page 90) or aloo dum (page 86) and a kachumber salad (page 305), or eat it rolled up in a nice warm paratha or chapati (page 306) with some of the wonderfully rich and hot juices. For a Sunday roast with a difference, serve it with the spiced roast potatoes and onions on page 306.
Recipe photograph overleaf

SERVES 8–10

40 dried Kashmiri chillies
200g ghee
1 whole leg of lamb on the
   bone weighing 2.25–2.75 kg
   (make sure you have a
   casserole big enough;
   if not, get your butcher
   to chop the leg in half)

200ml hot chicken
   stock or water
1 tsp salt

Preheat the oven to 150°C/Gas 2. Snip the stalks off the chillies with a pair of scissors. Remove and discard the seeds from 30 of the chillies. Leave the seeds in the remaining 10 chillies.

Put the ghee in a large, sturdy casserole dish and place over a medium heat. Once it's hot, add the lamb and brown for a few minutes on all sides, then add all the chillies and salt, and very carefully (as it may spit when it hits the fat) pour the hot stock or water over the lamb. Bring to a simmer, cover with a lid and transfer to the oven. Cook for 2–2½ hours, basting the lamb every half hour with the juices, and adding a splash more boiling water if it looks too dry (the bottom of the casserole should always be covered by at least 1cm liquid).

When cooked, the meat should be tender and almost falling off the bone and the liquid reduced to a rich sauce flavoured with the chillies, ghee and lamb juices; if it looks too thin, remove the lamb and keep it warm while you rapidly boil the juices over a high heat until reduced to a bubbling emulsion – stop reducing before it becomes all butter. Serve the lamb sliced or pulled off the bone with the chilli juices spooned on top.

ROAST SPICED WHOLE LEG OF LAMB FROM LUCKNOW
Raan mussallam

Another example of gloriously luxurious Mughal cooking. A whole leg of lamb is first marinated with garlic, ginger, yogurt, vinegar and spices, then gently braised for about 2 hours. This produces a moist, still slightly pink, slice. If you want it almost falling off the bone, then cook for another couple of hours, adding a splash more water to the roasting tin. The sort of Indian accompaniments would be a kachumber salad, naan bread and plain rice, but I actually like to serve it as a Sunday roast with roast potatoes, purple sprouting broccoli and carrots cooked in a little water with sugar, salt, butter and caraway seeds.

SERVES 6-8

2kg leg of lamb on the bone

For the spice paste
75ml vegetable oil
250g onions, thinly sliced
30g/6 cloves garlic,
    roughly chopped
30g/6cm ginger,
    roughly chopped
55g cashew nuts
75g desiccated coconut
300g thick Greek-style yogurt

3 tbsp red wine vinegar
2 tbsp *Garam masala* (page 303)
2 tsp salt
2 tsp Kashmiri chilli powder

To serve
Boiled basmati rice (page 313),
    Naan bread (page 306) and
    Kachumber salad (page 305),
    or serve as a British Sunday
    roast with all the trimmings
    (see introduction)

For the spice paste, heat the vegetable oil in a heavy-based saucepan or karahi over a medium heat and fry the onions for 10 minutes until deep golden brown. Add the garlic and ginger and fry for a further 2–3 minutes until golden. Transfer to a food processor, add all the remaining ingredients, blend to a paste and leave to cool.

Sit the leg of lamb in a roasting tin, prick all over with a small sharp knife, making incisions about 1.5cm deep, then rub two-thirds of the paste over the lamb, working it into the incisions. Set aside to marinate for 30 minutes.

Preheat the oven to 150°C/Gas 2. Put the remaining paste into the bottom of the roasting tin with 300ml water. Cover the tin loosely with foil and roast for 1½ hours, basting with the juices every 30 minutes and adding a splash of boiling water if it looks too dry. Then remove the foil and allow to roast uncovered for another 30 minutes. Remove from the oven and rest for 15 minutes before carving into fairly thick slices and serving Indian- or British-style.

WHITE LAMB CURRY
Safed maas

Safed means 'white' in most North Indian languages and is almost a complete opposite to another lamb dish, rogan josh (page 258); where that is deep red and spicy, this is off-white, very aromatic and mild. It would appear to come from somewhere like Lucknow, famed for rich, creamy dishes, but in fact it's a royal dish from Rajasthan, another region famed for its upper-class cookery. It's definitely from the same style of cooking as kormas and biryanis – fragrant and luxurious.

SERVES 6–8

For the spice blend
2 tbsp fennel seeds
1 tbsp green cardamom
    pods, seeds only
1 black cardamom pod,
    seeds only
1 tsp cloves
4cm piece of cinnamon stick
1 Indian bay leaf

For the lamb
100g cashew nuts
1 tbsp boiling water
1kg boneless lamb shoulder,
    cut into 4cm cubes

20g/4cm ginger, finely grated
25g/5 cloves garlic,
    finely crushed
100g thick Greek-style yogurt
150g ghee
1 small onion, sliced
1½ tsp salt
1 tsp ground cardamom
    (seeds from 30 green pods)
50ml double cream

To serve
Rick's everyday pilau rice
    (page 307) and *Chapatis*
    (page 306)

Fry the spices in a dry frying pan over a medium heat for 1–2 minutes until lightly toasted and aromatic, then blend to a powder (use a grinder or a pestle and mortar).

For the lamb, tip the cashew nuts and water into a mini food processor and blend to a paste. Set aside. Put the lamb in a large bowl and mix well with the spice blend, ginger, garlic and yogurt. Set aside to marinate for 30 minutes.

Heat the ghee in a sturdy, deep-sided pan over a low-medium heat and fry the onion for 5 minutes until softened but not browned. Add the meat and its marinade and pour in enough water to just cover the meat. Add the salt, bring to a simmer, cover and cook for 45 minutes to 1 hour, or until the lamb is tender and the sauce thickened. Stir in the cashew nut paste, ground cardamom and a splash of water if needed to give a sauce the consistency of double cream. Heat through, then stir in the cream and serve with chapattis and rice.

BEEF VINDALOO

I've chosen to use shin of beef here because it matches the beef in India, which can be pretty tough. This famous recipe from Goa calls for the overnight marination of the beef in vinegar and spices, and then a long, slow cooking till tender. The result is meat that falls apart and a rich, dark, thick sauce which has a delicious hot and sweet 'vinegariness'. This is the real thing, quite unlike those absurdly hot vindaloos you get in Indian restaurants in the UK. When filming in Bangladesh a few years ago, our guide told me that a couple of his friends from Sylhet with restaurants in the UK had been to my restaurant in Padstow, had the monkfish vindaloo and pronounced it not a vindaloo at all. I said nothing, but the recipe came from Rui Madre Deus, my friend in Baga Beach, Goa, and I reflected that I probably knew more about Goan vindaloo than they did. Of the dishes in the book, this is one of my favourites.

SERVES 6

RECIPE NOTE
The beef needs marinating for 12 hours or overnight.

750g boneless shin of beef, cut into 3cm-thick medallions

For the marinade
5cm piece of cinnamon stick
1 tsp black peppercorns
1 tsp cloves
1 tsp cumin seeds
Seeds from 12 green cardamoms
1 small onion, roughly chopped
40g/8 cloves garlic, peeled
25g/5cm ginger, roughly chopped
2 tbsp *Tamarind liquid* (page 313)

1½ tsp salt
½ tsp sugar
2 tbsp Kashmiri chilli powder
½ tsp turmeric
5 tbsp white wine vinegar

To cook the vindaloo
2 tbsp (30g) ghee or vegetable oil
1 small onion, chopped
3 medium, ripe tomatoes, sliced
3 fresh green chillies, halved lengthways, seeds removed
100ml water

For the marinade, grind the cinnamon, black peppercorns, cloves, cumin seeds and cardamom to a powder. Put the onion, garlic, ginger, tamarind, salt, sugar, chilli powder, turmeric and vinegar and all the ground spices into a mini food processor and blend together to a paste. Mix the beef and the paste together in a large bowl, coating the beef well. Cover the bowl and transfer to the fridge for 12 hours.

To cook the vindaloo, heat the ghee in a large, sturdy pan or casserole over a medium heat. Add the onion and fry for 10 minutes until golden. Increase the heat to medium-high, add the beef and all its marinade paste and fry for 5 minutes, stirring occasionally. Stir in the tomatoes, green chillies and water, cover with a lid and cook for around 2 hours until the meat is tender, checking every so often that it's not sticking or becoming dry, in which case add a splash of water. Serve.

BRITISH BEEF RAJ CURRY

I hadn't intended to include in this book any recipes that didn't come from India, but then I began thinking that as this is a collection of my favourite recipes, why not include one based on childhood memories of my mum's curries? Reading books on Anglo-Indian cuisine I saw that the essential difference between English curries and Indian is that the English curry is really based on a spiced version of a stew: the meat is browned first and then removed, then onions and garlic are browned, the meat returned, and spices are added with a good beef stock. The curry is finished with sultanas and served with a bowl of desiccated coconut and sliced banana and chutney. The only difference here is that I've added the desiccated coconut to the curry early on to give it what I consider to be a pleasant, grainy thickness. Funnily enough, the idea of adding fruit to meat curries is really quite common in India; see, for example, the chicken and apricot curry from Gujarat on page 198.

SERVES 4–6

25g butter
750g chuck steak,
   cut into 4cm cubes
2 medium onions, sliced
15g/3 cloves garlic, crushed
1 tsp Kashmiri chilli powder
1 tsp turmeric
1½ tbsp *Garam masala*
   (page 303)
1½ tsp salt
600ml beef stock
50g desiccated coconut
100g sultanas

To serve
Choose from: Bombay duck
   (or any dried, salted fish
   such as dried anchovies,
   available from Asian shops),
Apple chutney (page 304),
Tamarind chutney (page 304),
Kachumber Salad (page 305),
   sliced bananas, grated
   coconut, poppadoms

Melt the butter in a large, sturdy pan over a medium heat. Add the steak, in batches, and fry for a few minutes until browned, then remove to a plate. Add the onions to the same pan and fry for 10 minutes until softened and golden brown. Add the garlic and fry for 1 minute, then return the meat to the pan, along with any juices on the plate. Stir in the chilli powder, turmeric, 1 tablespoon of the garam masala, and the salt, and cook for 1 minute. Add the stock, followed by the coconut and sultanas. Bring to a simmer, cover and cook over a low heat for 45 minutes to an hour or until the beef is tender. Stir in the remaining garam masala and serve.

BIFE ASSADO

This is roast beef Goan-style (*assado* means 'roast' in Portuguese), and owing to the fact that Indians rarely use ovens, it's actually a pot roast. In Goa it's normal, having sliced the beef after a long, slow cooking, to fry it to give it a roasted flavour. But I simply slice it and serve it as I prefer the taste unfried, and there's so much flavour from the masala gravy anyway. I got this recipe from a chef chum, Atul Kochhar, whose restaurant Benares in London is the first Indian restaurant in the UK to get a Michelin star. Oddly enough, we were at the famous fish restaurant Mahesh in Juhu Tara Road in Mumbai talking about Mangalorean seafood when I said, 'You haven't got a recipe for Goan roast beef, have you? I like the sound of it.' And of course he had, and very good it is too.

SERVES 6-8

1.2kg piece beef or British veal – rump, silverside, topside or thick flank

For the spice marinade
25g/5 cloves garlic, finely crushed
25g/5cm piece ginger, finely grated
10 black peppercorns, crushed to a coarse powder
1 tsp turmeric
1 tsp ground cumin
1 tsp ground coriander
1 tsp salt
2 tbsp vegetable oil

For the beef
25g/5 cloves garlic, finely crushed
25g/5cm piece ginger, finely grated
1 tbsp wine or toddy vinegar
4 dried Kashmiri chillies
6 cloves
2 Indian bay leaves
5cm piece of cinnamon stick
1 litre water or beef stock
1½ tsp salt

To serve
Spiced roast potatoes (page 306) and your choice of vegetables

Prick the meat thoroughly all over with a small, sharp knife. Mix all the marinade ingredients together, rub over the meat and into the incisions and leave to marinate for one hour.

Put the beef in a large, heavy-based saucepan and add all the remaining ingredients. Bring to a simmer over a medium heat, then turn the heat to its lowest setting and simmer, covered, for 3–4 hours until the meat is tender, turning the meat every so often and basting with the juices, adding a splash more water if it looks dry.

Remove the beef from the cooking liquid. The liquid should be reduced to the consistency of single cream – if it's too thin then boil rapidly, uncovered, until reduced. Carve the beef into fairly thick slices, spoon over the sauce and serve.

AMMA'S PORK CURRY WITH GREEN CHILLIES AND TAMARIND

This is a Christian pork dish from Kerala, which to me is typical of the cookery of southern India in that, even though it's a meat dish, it's still light, fresh and acidic. The fattiness of pork is cut through by finishing the dish with a tamarind paste, sliced green chillies and garlic, and it's normal to serve a sliced, pickled onion salad with it as well.

SERVES 6-8

For the curry
6 large banana shallots, sliced
100g/20 cloves garlic, peeled
30g/6cm ginger, finely chopped
6 green chillies, roughly
  chopped, with or without
  seeds according to preference
1 tbsp black mustard seeds
1 tsp cumin seeds
2 cloves
4cm piece of cinnamon stick
½ tsp black peppercorns
1 tsp turmeric
2 tbsp vegetable oil

1kg boneless pork shoulder or
  chops, cut into 4cm chunks
1 tsp salt

To finish
2 tsp coriander seeds
75ml *Tamarind liquid*
  (page 313)
3 green chillies, thinly sliced
  lengthways, without seeds
25g/5 cloves garlic, thinly sliced
Flash pickled onion and
  pineapple salad (page 305),
  to serve

Put the shallots, garlic, ginger and chillies into a mini food processor with a splash of water and blend to a rough paste.

Fry the mustard seeds, cumin, cloves, cinnamon stick and peppercorns in a dry frying pan over a medium heat for a minute until toasted and aromatic. Add the turmeric and fry for another 20 seconds. Cool, then grind to a coarse powder.

Heat the oil in a heavy-based pan or karahi over a medium-high heat. Add the pork, in batches if necessary to avoid overcrowding, and fry for 10 minutes, stirring occasionally, until browned. With all the pork in the pan, add the shallot, garlic, ginger and chilli paste, the ground spices and salt, and fry for a further 5 minutes, adding a splash of water if the paste starts to stick. Pour over enough water to just cover, turn the heat down to low, put a lid on and simmer for about 30 minutes, or until the meat is tender.

To finish, fry the coriander seeds in a dry frying pan over a medium heat for a minute until toasted, then grind to a powder. Add the tamarind liquid, green chillies and garlic to the pork and cook for a further minute, then stir in the ground coriander. Serve with the salad on the side.

MEETHA

...kulfi, nimish and some other indulgent Indian sweets

I observe an interesting paradox when talking to Europeans about Indian sweets. The general opinion is that they are far too sweet and far too rich and not for them. The actuality, I notice, from staying in many large hotels in Calcutta, Lucknow, Mumbai and Chennai, is that virtually everyone goes up for seconds at the buffet. Yes, they are ridiculously sweet and yes, they are full of yogurt, milk and cream, but you can't resist them. You do have to make a little bit of a sugar adjustment to, say, a jalebi on a street corner: it's just a flour, semolina and yogurt batter flavoured with saffron dropped in a squiggle into hot oil, scooped out when crisp, and then dunked into a bath of the sweetest rosewater and cardamom syrup and served to you on a little square of greaseproof paper. The sensation is simply almost too much to bear; it is the contrast of the crispness and the softening effect of the syrup – you just have to have another. Maybe, if you're lucky, you can pick up a glass of very sweet masala chai – a milky tea made with black tea leaves, cardamom, cloves and cinnamon – and then the tea will taste almost unsweetened in contrast to the jalebis.

Kulfi, too, can seem very rich and sweet. It's an ice cream made from milk flavoured with cardamom that has been simmered for a long time so it becomes thick and slightly grainy – this is a normal way of making a dish creamy, as with the payasam on page 296. They don't generally use cream in India; it's either milk or yogurt. You can make kulfi by using evaporated milk, but there is something about the flavour when you take the trouble to reduce fresh milk yourself that makes it much more satisfying. To start with, the chewy graininess seems an imperfection, and then you realize it is the most desirable part.

Nimish – what a lovely name – is a mere whimsy as well. It's simply whipped, sweetened cream and milk, flavoured with saffron and rosewater. I remember walking through the cool streets of Lucknow at dawn and stopping at a stall with a giant bowl full of it, scattered with saffron, pistachio nuts and silver leaf. They scooped up a glassful for me, and I thought about how traditionally the dish, made only in the cool winter months, contains the morning dew which settles on the cream and the rim of the earthenware milk pan left out in the open. That to me was to experience the mystique of India in a single taste.

I've also included a couple of drinks that I particularly enjoy: masala chai, of course, but also a fresh lime and ginger cordial from Kerala, served like they used to deliver citron pressé in Parisian cafés: a jug of freshly squeezed lime juice, puréed ginger and sugar and a bottle of ice-cold sparkling mineral water. The most refreshing of drinks on a hot, tropical day.

BREAD AND BUTTER PUDDING INDIAN-STYLE
Shahi tukra

With its origins in the imperial kitchens of the Mughal Empire, shahi tukra
rather outshines our own bread and butter pudding. As with so many Indian
sweets, people gasp in horror at the prodigious amount of sugar, ghee and cream
they involve. Yet I could not help noticing on my travels with the TV crew that
return trips to the pudding department of the buffet were frequent and happy.
I particularly like the way the bread is fried in ghee first. It gives the dish a
comforting, toasty butteriness.

SERVES 8

RECIPE NOTE
Make the day before
you plan to serve it.

Vegetable oil or ghee
   for shallow frying
8 slices white bread,
   crusts removed,
   cut in half diagonally
750ml whole milk
75g caster sugar
6 green cardamom pods,
   lightly bruised with
   a rolling pin

¼ tsp saffron strands,
   soaked in 2 tsp warm
   water for 15 minutes
3 tbsp double cream
1 tsp rosewater, or to taste
1 tbsp pistachio nuts
   and/or blanched
   almonds, thinly sliced
2 tbsp sultanas, covered in
   boiling water, soaked for
   15 minutes then drained

Heat a 2cm depth of oil or ghee in a sturdy, deep-sided pan over a medium heat. Once
hot, fry the bread in batches until golden on both sides, then drain on kitchen paper.

   Pour the milk into a wide, shallow pan over a medium heat and stir in the sugar
and cardamom pods. Simmer for 5 minutes, or until reduced in volume by a third.
Stir in the saffron and its soaking water, the cream and rosewater, then lower the
bread into the hot milk and simmer gently for 1–2 minutes. Transfer the softened
bread to a serving dish and pour over any remaining milk. Leave to cool then chill
in the fridge overnight. Garnish with nuts and sultanas and serve.

DILIP BAKERY
Ph 2352-4683
Special Sheed Bread
CAKE&BUNS
41. N. N. ROAD. Kolka

NIMISH

This is a light, set cream from Lucknow flavoured with saffron and rosewater
– a typical sweet from the era of the Nawabs and their very inventive chefs. It is
standard practice to present the nimish covered with silver leaf as well as pistachios.
Due to the almost unbearable heat in Lucknow in the summer, it's a dish only produced
in the cooler winter months; actually, the season only lasts when there is dew on
the grass. I had heard that nimish incorporated the early morning dew and assumed
this was a bit of romantic frippery, but it's true: they do collect the dew at night
and in the morning whisk it into the cream and milk.

SERVES 6-8

RECIPE NOTE
Make the day before
you plan to serve it.

450g double cream
50g icing sugar
1 tsp rosewater
Pinch of saffron strands,
    soaked in 100ml warm
    milk for 15 minutes

To decorate
Few chopped pistachios and
    edible silver leaf (optional)

Whip the cream until soft peaks just start to form – it's important not to over-whisk
it. Sift in the icing sugar then add the rosewater and the now cool saffron milk and
strands. Whisk together for a minute until smooth and a few bubbles appear on
the surface. Pour gently into small serving bowls or glasses and chill overnight.
Decorate with sliced pistachios, and silver leaf if you like. Serve.

SWEET YELLOW RICE WITH NUTS AND DRIED FRUIT FROM THE DHAM FESTIVAL

This is not a creamy rice pudding like we're used to, but it's deliciously buttery and coconutty, infused with saffron and finished with cashews, pistachios, almonds and raisins, which have all been fried in a generous dollop of ghee. I found this dish at a dham, a festival day in Himachal Pradesh. This one was an occasion in the village of Lambagaon where the ruling family of the area, the Katochs, invite the whole village to come and eat with them.

SERVES 6

For the ghee-fried fruit and nuts
75g ghee
25g cashew nuts
25g pistachios
25g blanched almonds
25g raisins

For the yellow rice
4 cloves
4 green cardamom pods, lightly bruised with a rolling pin
3cm piece of cinnamon stick, broken up
350g basmati rice
500ml cold water
200g sugar
50g desiccated coconut
160ml can coconut cream
Generous pinch of saffron, soaked in 50ml warm milk

Heat the ghee in a large, heavy-based saucepan over a medium heat. Add the cashew nuts, pistachios, almonds and raisins and fry for 2–3 minutes until lightly toasted. Remove with a slotted spoon, leaving most of the ghee in the pan, and set aside.

Add the cloves, cardamom pods and cinnamon stick to the ghee and fry for 1 minute, then stir in the basmati rice and cook in the ghee for about a minute. Pour in the water, sugar, desiccated coconut, coconut cream and the saffron milk, bring to the boil, stir once, lower the heat, cover and cook for 12–15 minutes without stirring, until the rice has absorbed all the water and is cooked. Very gently fold through the fried fruit and nuts, saving a few for decoration. Spoon into serving bowls and scatter with remaining fruit and nuts.

CARDAMOM SHORTBREAD
WITH CHILLED MANGO FOOL

I got the recipe for these deliciously crumbly shortbreads flavoured with cardamom from a cardamom and pepper farm in the Western Ghat mountains. After we'd had a couple of them with a cup of local tea, Gita Eapen gave me the recipe, from an old Keralan cookery book, when we were all secretly hoping she would produce the tin again. They were so good I thought I'd combine them with a very simple recipe of my own for mangoes in a fool with yogurt and cream. *Recipe photograph overleaf*

SERVES 6

RECIPE NOTE
Makes at least
18 biscuits, which
will keep in an
airtight container
for 3–4 days.

For the cardamom shortbreads
100g ghee
100g icing sugar
125g plain flour
Scant ¼ tsp baking powder
Pinch of salt
2 green cardamom pods,
    seeds only, finely ground

For the chilled mango fool
300g fresh mango flesh
1½ tbsp lemon juice
150g natural yogurt
200g double cream
75g caster sugar
Zest of 1 lime, to serve

Preheat the oven to 160°C/Gas 3. Put the ghee into a large mixing bowl and use hand-held electric beaters to whisk it until white and creamy. Beat in the icing sugar, then sift in the flour, baking powder, salt and cardamom and mix well until the ingredients come together into a dough.

Roll the dough to a thickness of about 1cm, and use a small round cutter, about 4cm, to stamp out biscuits. Transfer to non-stick baking sheets (or baking sheets lined with baking parchment), leaving a little room between each one.

Bake for 15 minutes, until firm and light golden – take care not to brown them. Cool on the baking sheets then transfer to an airtight container until ready to serve.

For the chilled mango fool, blend the mango to a purée in a food processor or using a stick blender. In a large mixing bowl, mix the mango purée with the lemon juice and the yogurt.

Pour the cream and caster sugar into a separate bowl and whisk to soft peaks.

Fold the cream though the mango and yogurt mixture then spoon into 6 small serving dishes or glasses and chill for at least an hour. Just before serving with the shortbread, finely grate the zest of the lime over the top.

COCONUT, CARDAMOM AND PISTACHIO LADOO

These gobstopper balls of condensed milk and coconut, flavoured with saffron and rolled in more coconut and chopped pistachios, are extremely hard to leave alone. The recipe calls for only half a tin of condensed milk. Keep the other half in your store cupboard for sweetening masala chai (page 297). *Recipe photograph overleaf*

MAKES ABOUT 20

200g (½ tin) sweetened condensed milk
200g desiccated coconut
8 cardamom pods, finely crushed seeds only
Small pinch of saffron threads, soaked in 1 tbsp warm milk for 15 minutes

To coat
50g desiccated coconut
25g pistachios, finely chopped
Pinch of salt flakes, to sprinkle

In a bowl mix together the condensed milk, coconut, cardamom and saffron milk. Tip into a non-stick frying pan and stir over a medium heat for about 5 minutes until the mixture comes away from the sides of the pan. Remove from the heat and set aside until cool enough to handle.

Dip your hands in water then take just under a tablespoon of the mixture and roll it into a ball. Roll it in the extra coconut and chopped pistachios. Continue until the mixture is used up. Chill in the fridge for about an hour before serving, or serve at room temperature. Sprinkle with a pinch of salt before serving.

JALEBI

As with many Indian sweets, one gets a little addicted to jalebi. I suppose you could call them just plain naughty. A swirl of batter flavoured with saffron, deep-fried till crisp then dropped into the sweetest of sugar syrups with more saffron, cardamom and rosewater, and eaten while they're a bit soft and a bit crisp. Lovely. The recipe comes from a chef friend of mine in Australia, Christine Manfield, whose book *Tasting India* makes you never want to write another cookery book, particularly about India, because it's so overwhelmingly splendid. *Recipe photograph overleaf*

MAKES ABOUT 25

For the batter
250g plain flour
1½ tbsp semolina
½ tsp baking powder
2 tbsp natural yogurt
¼ tsp salt
300ml warm water
½ tsp saffron

For the syrup
600g caster sugar
800ml water
Pinch of saffron
½ tsp ground cardamom
   (seeds from 15 green pods)
1½ tbsp rosewater
Vegetable or sunflower
   oil, for deep-frying

Combine the flour, semolina, baking powder, yogurt, salt and half the warm water in a bowl. Whisk well, then add the remaining water and saffron and set aside for 30 minutes.

To make the syrup, dissolve the caster sugar in the water in a pan, simmer for 5 minutes, then add the saffron and cardamom. Finally stir in the rosewater.

To cook the jalebis, heat enough oil for deep-frying to 160°C. Add the batter directly to the hot oil in a steady stream in a spiral shape about 7cm in diameter (I use a squeezy chef's sauce bottle to do this, or you could use a piping bag with a thin nozzle). Make a few at a time and fry for 3–5 minutes until crisp and golden all over, but not brown. Remove with a slotted spoon and drain on kitchen paper.

Immerse them in the warm syrup for 4–5 minutes so that the jalebis soak it up. Remove from the syrup and serve warm.

CASHEW AND JAGGERY KULFI SCENTED WITH CARDAMOM

Though you can find kulfi everywhere in India, it more often tastes to me just like vanilla ice cream flavoured with cardamom. In this recipe I've taken a large volume of milk and reduced it carefully down until it's thick. This requires some patience to stop it catching, but is well worth it. I've added cardamom, cashew nuts and jaggery. It is much more than a mere ice cream. Its texture is fascinating.

SERVES 6

RECIPE NOTE
Make the day before you plan to serve it.

60g cashew nuts
1 litre whole milk
410g can evaporated milk
½ tsp ground cardamom
 (seeds from 15 green pods)

100g jaggery or light
 soft brown sugar
50g caster sugar
Pinch of salt (⅛ tsp)

Tip the cashew nuts into a frying pan and toast over a medium heat for 3–4 minutes until lightly golden. Leave to cool, then chop finely and set aside.

Put the milk, evaporated milk and cardamom into a large, heavy-based saucepan or karahi over a medium heat, bring to the boil, then lower the heat to low-medium and simmer for 1 hour and 15 minutes, or until reduced by about half, stirring occasionally, incorporating the skin and scraping down the sides of the pan every now and then. Stir in the jaggery, caster sugar and salt, and simmer for a further 10 minutes, keeping a close eye on it and stirring regularly to make sure it doesn't catch on the bottom of the pan. Stir in 50g of the cashew nuts. Leave to cool then pour into small (about 150ml) kulfi moulds, pots or freezer-proof glasses, filling each about two-thirds full. Freeze overnight. Remove from the freezer about 5 minutes before serving. Serve frozen in their pots or turned out on to small plates, scattered with the remaining cashew nuts.

SWEET MILK PUDDING WITH VERMICELLI
Payasam

This is a very typical Tamil dessert; it will always be served at a Tamil wedding. A wedding that doesn't serve payasam is not a real wedding, according to the locals. It's slowly cooked milk reduced to the thickness of double cream and set with vermicelli and cardamom, decorated with pistachios, cashews and sultanas. As with the majority of Indian sweets, best to eat them in small portions as they're very rich, but worth it every time.

SERVES 4-6

RECIPE NOTE
Make the day before you plan to serve it.

1 litre whole milk
1 tsp ghee or butter
50g vermicelli, broken
    into rough 4cm pieces
4 tbsp sugar
¼ tsp ground cardamom
    (or seeds from 8 pods)

To decorate
1 tbsp ghee or butter
25g cashew nuts
25g pistachio nuts
25g sultanas

Pour the milk into a large, deep-sided pan or karahi and place over a medium-high heat until it comes to the boil, then reduce the heat slightly and simmer for about 20 minutes until reduced in volume by a third.

Meanwhile, heat the ghee in a pan over a medium heat, add the vermicelli and fry for 1–2 minutes until lightly toasted but not browned.

Once the milk has reduced, add the toasted vermicelli to the milk and simmer for a further 20 minutes until the vermicelli is soft and the milk reduced further. Stir in the sugar and cardamom, leave to cool slightly then pour into a serving dish or individual bowls or glasses.

To decorate, heat the ghee in a pan over a medium heat, add the cashew nuts and pistachio nuts and fry for 2–3 minutes until golden, then stir in the sultanas. Spoon over the payasam, leave to cool, then transfer to the fridge to chill – overnight is best. Serve in small portions.

MASALA CHAI

Is there anything more satisfying on earth after a large dinner of curries than a whole teapot full of sweet, milky tea fragrant with cardamom, cinnamon and cloves? This is the famous spicy tea now catching on everywhere. The recipe varies enormously. What I generally discovered was that ginger is the predominant flavour in the summer months and cardamom in the winter.

MAKES 2 BIG MUGS OR 4–6 SMALL CHAI GLASSES

1 black cardamom pod, bruised with a rolling pin
15 green cardamom pods, bruised with a rolling pin
6 cloves
4 black peppercorns
8cm piece of cinnamon stick, broken in half

500ml water
4 tsp black tea leaves (from about 2 tea bags if using bags)
2 tsp sugar, plus extra to taste
200ml milk

Put the spices into a saucepan with the water. Bring to a boil, add the tea and turn down the heat to low and simmer for 7 minutes. Stir in the sugar and milk, bring back to a simmer for 3 minutes. Strain through a fine strainer and serve, adding more sugar to taste.

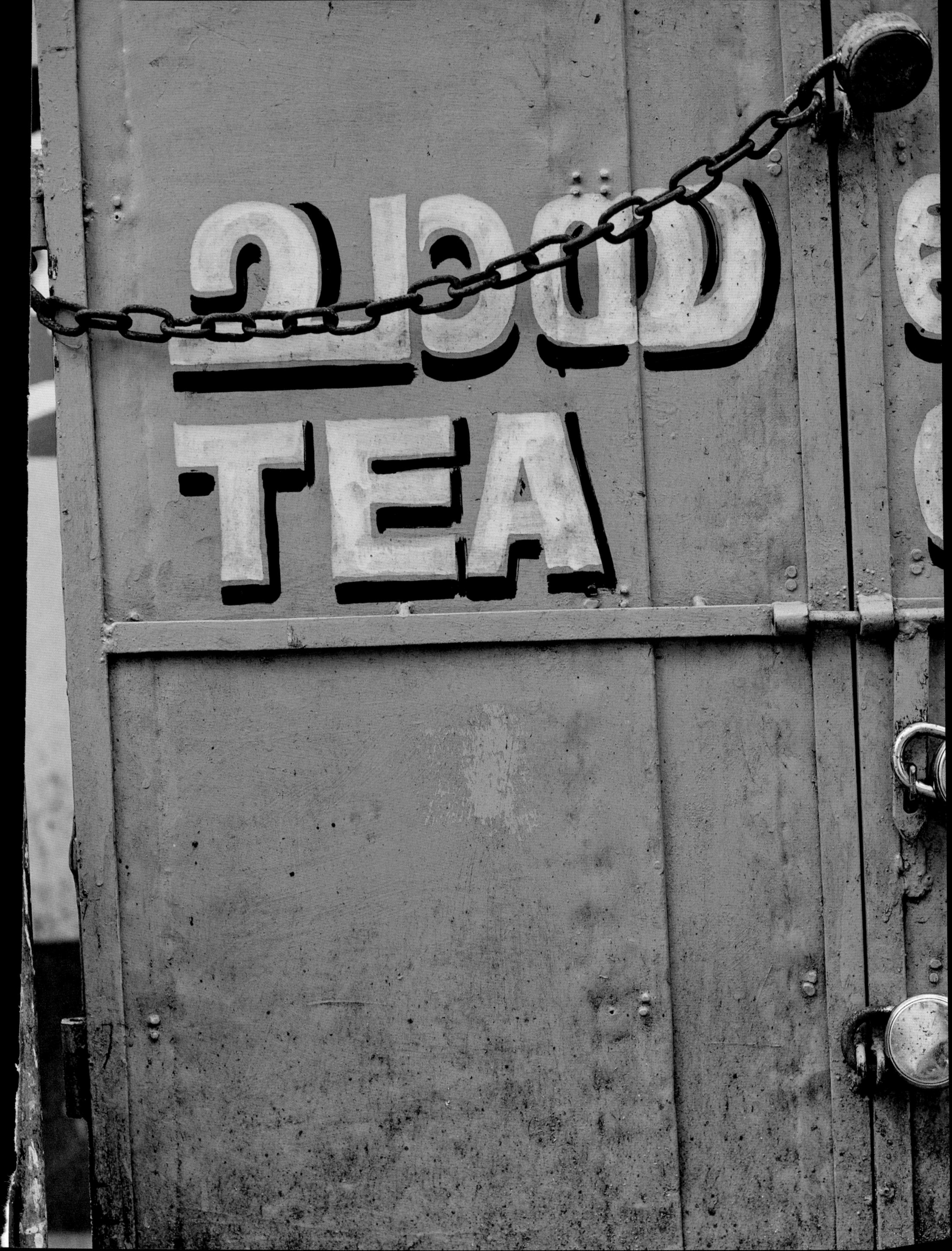
TEA

LIME AND GINGER CORDIAL

I got this idea from a restaurant called the Ginger House in the heart of Jew Town in Cochin. They supplied a jug of ginger lime syrup and a separate jug of soda water so you could make it up at your leisure.

MAKES ABOUT 500ML

For the cordial
250g sugar
300ml boiling water
20g ginger, washed and
    roughly chopped (no need
    to peel as long as it's washed)
Juice of 8–10 limes (120ml)
Zest of 2 limes

To serve
Ice and soda water

In a heatproof jug, dissolve the sugar in the water then stir in the ginger. Leave to cool slightly then transfer to a blender with the lime juice and blend until smooth. Pass through a sieve, stir in the lime zest and chill until ready to serve.

Pour over ice and top up with soda water.

EXTRAS

CHAT MASALA

Makes 50–75g
Keeps for about 1 month

There are more mixtures of spices called masalas in India than you can shake a stick at. On the whole I've chosen spices appropriate for each curry but there are two spice mixtures that must be included in this book. First, naturally garam masala (see right), but also chat masala. The most important ingredients of this are black salt and amchur, which gives the masala a surprising tanginess. These days I couldn't possibly eat my tandoori fish (page 179) without a sprinkling of chat masala. It livens up many a dal in northern India, and the liberal sprinkling of it on my Amritsari fish (page 164) is going to knock 'em dead at the seafood restaurant in Padstow.

1 tbsp cumin seeds
1 tbsp coriander seeds
1 tbsp black peppercorns
1 tbsp amchur (dried
　　green mango powder)
1 tbsp dried ginger powder
1 tsp asafoetida
1 tbsp Kashmiri chilli powder
1 tbsp black salt powder
　　or pieces
1 tbsp salt

Roast the cumin, coriander and black pepper in a dry frying pan over a medium heat for 1–2 minutes or until lightly toasted and fragrant. Cool, then combine all the ingredients in a spice mixer or pestle and mortar and make a fine powder. Store in a sealed container out of the sunlight.

GARAM MASALA

Makes 50g
Keeps for about 1 month

This is my own garam masala recipe, which is essentially a balanced combination of the most popular spices. Even more important than the mix is having them freshly roasted and ground. I can't stress too strongly how much better it is to make your own garam masala than to buy it. You may be astonished about the number of times garam masala turns up in the book; sometimes it's the only spice in a dish. But this mixture represents perfect balance to me, and the reason it appears so often is because once you've made it, it's easy to knock up a large number of recipes without resorting to teaspoons of this and that. It's important to make this regularly; I would suggest renewing it every month. Keep it in an airtight container.

1 tbsp black peppercorns
2 tbsp cumin seeds
2 tbsp coriander seeds
2 tsp cardamom seeds
　　(from 30–40 green pods)
4 tsp whole cloves
7cm piece of cinnamon stick
1 whole nutmeg

Roast all the spices apart from the nutmeg in a dry frying pan over a medium heat for a couple of minutes until toasted and aromatic. Cool. Grate the nutmeg and add to a spice grinder along with whole spices (you might want to break up the cinnamon stick) and grind everything to a fine powder. Store in a sealed container out of the sunlight; it will keep its most aromatic condition for a month.

GREEN CHUTNEY

Serves about 6
Eat freshly made

Far too often this green chutney is not freshly made in India, and it only works when it is. I've taken the liberty of adding a tad more sugar than most but it doesn't half work well with the lime juice. I can't think of a curry that it doesn't go with.

Large handful of mint leaves
Large handful of coriander leaves
2 fresh green chillies,
　　roughly chopped
1 small onion (75g),
　　roughly chopped
1½ tsp sugar
¼ tsp ground cumin
2 tsp lime juice
¼ tsp salt

Tip all the ingredients into a food processor and blend to a rough paste.

TIBETAN CHILLI SAUCE

Makes about 10 portions
Keeps for a few days in the fridge

This is fiery, vinegary and pungent with garlic. Essential with a momo (page 20), tingmo (page 22) or to liven up a thukpa (page 56).

13 dried Kashmiri chillies
50g/10 cloves garlic, peeled
3 tbsp rice vinegar
1 tbsp vegetable oil
1 tsp sugar
¼ tsp salt
2 tbsp water

Snip the stalks off the chillies using scissors, but leave the seeds. Place the chillies in a mini food processor with all the remaining ingredients and blend to a paste.

CHILLI GARLIC RELISH

Makes about 10 portions
Keeps for a week in the fridge
I absolutely can't remember where this came from, but it's very good, particularly with my spicy scrambled eggs (page 34). Like all relishes and chutneys, it's there to provide a good contrast of flavours.

3 large bulbs garlic, separated into individual cloves and peeled
5 tbsp water
3 tbsp vegetable oil
2 tsp black mustard seeds
1 tsp turmeric
¾ tsp Kashmiri chilli powder
¾ tsp salt

Put the garlic in a mini food processor with the water and blend to a coarse paste. Heat the vegetable oil in a frying pan over a medium heat, then add the mustard seeds – they will pop and spit as they release their flavour into the oil. After about 30 seconds turn the heat to low, add the turmeric and chilli powder and fry for another 30 seconds. Stir in the garlic and salt and fry, stirring often, for 3–4 minutes, until the garlic turns golden and smells aromatic. Turn off the heat and leave to cool to room temperature.

TAMARIND CHUTNEY

Makes about 6 portions
Keeps for a few days in the fridge
This is a British Raj chutney that goes very well with any lamb curry.

20g butter
2 tbsp black mustard seeds
35g/7cm ginger, finely grated
2 fresh green chillies, finely chopped, with seeds
2 tbsp *Tamarind liquid* (page 313)
¼ tsp salt

Melt the butter in a small frying pan over a medium heat, add the mustard seeds and fry for 1 minute until they start popping, then tip into a bowl and stir in all the other ingredients.

COCONUT CHUTNEY

Serves 4
Eat on the day of making
75g grated coconut
1 fresh green chilli, chopped, with seeds
1 shallot, chopped
15g/3cm ginger, chopped
½ tsp salt
For a tarka (optional)
1 tbsp vegetable oil
10 fresh curry leaves
1 dried Kashmiri chilli, torn into small pieces

Put everything into a mini food processor and blend to a coarse paste, adding a splash of water if needed to loosen. Serve.

For the optional tarka, heat the oil in a karahi over a medium heat, add the curry leaves and red chilli, fry for a minute or two then spoon over the chutney.

CUCUMBER AND MINT RAITA

Serves 10
Eat on the day of making
175g unpeeled cucumber, halved lengthways
1 tsp salt
275g natural yogurt
½ tsp caster sugar
3 tbsp chopped fresh mint leaves
Freshly ground black pepper
1 tsp fresh lime juice

Scoop out the seeds from the cucumber using a teaspoon, then grate. Toss the cucumber with the salt, tip into a sieve and leave to drain for 20–30 minutes. Mix the drained cucumber with all the remaining ingredients, adding a little extra salt, pepper or lime juice to taste.

APPLE CHUTNEY

Serves 10
Eat on the day of making
This is not, strictly speaking, Indian, but influenced by similar Indian chutneys. I like it because I like my vinegar, which is not much used there. Great with any meat dish.

2 Cox's apples
1 small onion
1 fresh green chilli, finely chopped, with seeds
Handful of parsley, finely chopped
2 tbsp white wine vinegar
¼ tsp salt

Coarsely grate the apple and onion and mix together with all the remaining ingredients.

BEETROOT CHUTNEY

Serves 15/Eat on the day of making
A recipe from Constance Spry's cookery book, my mother's favourite.

2 medium (tennis-ball-sized) raw beetroot, coarsely grated
1 tbsp hot horseradish from a jar (not creamed)
1 tbsp white wine vinegar
¼ tsp salt

Mix everything together.

MUSTARD CHUTNEY (KASUNDI)

Serves 4
Keeps for a few days in the fridge
It's a bit of an acquired taste, but it's a taste I have now acquired and so it's in the book. Serve with the prawn fritters on page 40.

4 tbsp black mustard seeds, soaked in 100ml water for 5 hours
1 fresh green chilli, roughly chopped
10g/2 cloves garlic, roughly chopped
15g/3cm ginger, roughly chopped
½ tsp turmeric
½ tsp sugar
½ tsp salt
1 tbsp lime juice

Tip the mustard seeds along with their water into a mini food processor, add all the other ingredients apart from the lime juice, and blend to a paste. Stir in the lime juice and serve.

RICK'S TOMATO CHUTNEY

Makes about 10 portions
Keeps for 2 weeks in the fridge
This has the intensity and thickness of tomato ketchup but with lots of spice. Serve with anything you want to add a hot sweet kick to. It goes with Keralan dishes like sambar or thoran, and I like it with the dry Chettinad chicken on page 216.

50ml mustard oil or vegetable oil
10 fresh curry leaves
1 tsp black mustard seeds
1 tsp cumin seeds
1 tbsp split urid dal or other split pea
50g onion, chopped
5g/1 clove garlic, thinly sliced
15g/3cm ginger, thinly sliced
1 tsp Kashmiri chilli powder
1 tsp ground coriander
¼ tsp turmeric
2 tsp sugar
1 tsp salt
1 fresh green chilli, chopped
1 x 400g tin tomatoes

Heat the oil in a karahi over a medium heat, add the curry leaves, mustard and cumin seeds and urid dal and fry for a minute or two. Add the onion and fry for 5 minutes or until softened and golden, then add the garlic and ginger and fry for a further 2 minutes. Stir in the ground spices, sugar and salt and cook for 30 seconds to 1 minute, then stir in the green chilli and tomatoes. Bring to a simmer and cook over low-medium heat for 20 minutes. Leave to cool slightly then tip into a blender or use a stick blender and blend to a purée. Serve cold.

SWEET MANGO CHUTNEY

Makes about 10 portions
Keeps for 2 weeks in the fridge
I'm still a fan of British mango chutney. This is similarly sweet but it's slightly sharper too, and the slices of mango are a little firmer. Great with any lamb curry.

100g sugar
100ml white wine vinegar
300g mango flesh (from firm mangoes), cut into 2cm slices
1 small onion, finely chopped
10g/2cm ginger, finely grated
5g/1 clove garlic, finely crushed
1 tsp whole cumin seeds
1 tsp ground Kashmiri chilli
½ tsp salt

Pour the sugar and vinegar into a pan and stir to dissolve over a medium heat. Add all the remaining ingredients and simmer over low-medium heat, stirring occasionally, for 45 minutes to an hour, or until reduced down to a jammy consistency.

KACHUMBER SALAD

Serves 8–10
300g vine-ripened tomatoes, thinly sliced
½ cucumber, sliced
100g red onions, halved and thinly sliced
1 fresh green chilli, finely chopped
½ tsp toasted ground cumin seeds
¼ tsp Kashmiri chilli powder
Large handful of fresh coriander leaves, roughly chopped
Freshly ground black pepper
1 tbsp freshly squeezed lime juice or white wine vinegar
Lime wedges (optional), to finish

Layer the ingredients, or gently toss together, just before serving. Serve with lime wedges, if desired.

FLASH PICKLED ONION AND PINEAPPLE SALAD

Serves 4–6
From Philipkutty's Farm, a quick colourful salad to cut through rich or fatty dishes. Ideal with pork curries.

1 small red onion, thinly sliced into rounds
2 tbsp white wine vinegar
½ tsp sugar
½ tsp salt
300g pineapple, peeled and cut into 2cm pieces
A few fresh coriander leaves, roughly chopped

Toss the onions together with the vinegar, sugar and salt and leave to marinate for an hour. Strain off any excess liquid, then toss the onions with the pineapple chunks, scatter with coriander and serve.

CRISP FRIED ONIONS

Serves about 10
Use to garnish rice dishes such as biryani or pulao, or to scatter over slow-cooked or roast meat dishes. Particularly good with the duck roast on page 222.

Vegetable oil
2 medium onions, thinly sliced
Salt

Heat about 2cm of vegetable oil in a heavy-based pan or karahi over a medium-high heat. Add the onions and fry, stirring now and then, until crisp and golden. Remove with a slotted spoon and drain on kitchen paper. Sprinkle with a little salt.

SPICED ROAST POTATOES AND ONIONS

Serves 6

Achamma Thomas is a home-cook who lives on a rural rubber-tree plantation in Kerala. Her recipe for duck roast on page 222 is exquisite, and she served it with onions and potatoes fried in coconut oil. I also found that roasting the potatoes worked well. This would make a really good side dish with other roasts, especially the lamb on page 264.

1kg potatoes, peeled and cut
   into 4cm x 1cm-thick pieces
2 large onions, sliced
2 sprigs fresh curry leaves
2 tsp Kashmiri chilli powder
1 tsp turmeric
1 tsp salt
6 tbsp vegetable oil

Preheat the oven to 180°C/Gas 4. Boil the potatoes in a large pan of salted water for 4 minutes until just tender, then drain thoroughly and tip them into a large roasting tin. Toss with the onions, curry leaves, chilli powder, turmeric, salt and oil. Roast for 45 minutes to 1 hour, until crisp and golden.

CHAPATIS

Makes 8

250g chapati flour, or half
   wholemeal, half plain white
   flour, plus extra for dusting
½ tsp salt
2 tbsp melted ghee, butter
   or vegetable oil, plus
   extra for brushing
120–150ml warm water

In a mixing bowl, mix the flour with the salt, then add the melted ghee or oil and 120ml of the water. Mix together, adding a little more water if needed, until you have a soft but not sticky dough. Knead in the bowl for a minute or two then cover and leave to rest for 15 minutes.

Divide the dough into 8 pieces. On a lightly floured surface, roll each piece into a ball then use a lightly floured rolling pin to roll out into a circle about 13cm in diameter.

Heat a heavy-based frying pan or griddle over a medium heat. When hot, place one of the circles of dough in the pan and cook for 1–2 minutes, or until bubbles appear on the surface and it puffs up. Flip the bread over, press down with a spatula so that it cooks evenly, and cook for a further minute, or until the bread is golden-brown.

Remove from the pan and put on a warm plate covered by a tea towel to keep warm while you cook the rest. Brush with a little melted ghee, butter or vegetable oil if you like, or leave plain. Serve warm.

NAAN

Makes 6

200g plain flour, plus
   extra for dusting
100g strong plain bread flour
1 tsp sugar
1½ tsp fast-action
   (easy-blend) yeast
1 tsp salt
100ml milk
100ml water
4 tbsp natural yogurt
2 tbsp melted ghee, butter
   or vegetable oil
For garlic butter naans (optional)
50g ghee or butter, melted
10g/2 cloves garlic, finely crushed

Sift the flours, sugar, yeast and salt into a large mixing bowl. Warm the milk and water together in a small pan to blood temperature (38°C). Add the yogurt and melted ghee or oil to the dry ingredients, followed by the warm milk and water mixture, and gradually mix everything together, adding a little more warm water if necessary, to make a soft, pliable dough. Turn out on to a lightly floured work surface and knead for 5 minutes until smooth. Return the dough to a clean bowl, cover and leave somewhere warm for up to 1 hour until it has doubled in size.

Turn the dough out on to a lightly floured surface and knead once more for about 5 minutes until smooth and elastic. Divide into 6 evenly sized pieces.

Roll out the first piece of dough thinly into a teardrop shape, about 25cm x 12cm. Heat your largest frying pan and drop the naan into it. Don't use oil. When it starts to puff up, turn it over. Total cooking time will be about 5 minutes. I like it to get a little scorched on each side. Alternatively, use a baking tray on the heat or in a hot oven, or, if you like pans, buy a large, round, flat Indian tawa.

Put on a warm plate covered by a tea towel, and continue to make the rest of the breads in the same way. For garlic butter naans, mix the melted ghee or butter with the garlic and spread over the naans when serving.

PARATHAS

Makes 8

The paratha is a flaky version of the chapati. Made with the same dough, it is the rolling out to create a few layers that gives it the flaky texture.

250g chapati flour, or half
wholemeal, half plain white
flour, plus extra for dusting
½ tsp salt
2 tbsp melted ghee or butter,
plus extra 5 tbsp for brushing
120–150ml warm water

In a mixing bowl, mix the flour
with the salt, then add the melted
ghee or oil and 120ml of the
water. Mix together, adding a
little more water if needed, until
you have a soft but not sticky
dough. Knead in the bowl for a
minute or two then cover and
leave to rest for 15 minutes.

Divide the dough into 8 pieces.
On a lightly floured surface, roll
each piece into a ball then use
a lightly floured rolling pin to
roll out into a circle about 13cm
in diameter. Brush the top with
melted ghee or butter and dust
with a little flour. Fold in half to
form a half moon (enclosing the
butter), then brush the top with
more ghee or butter and dust with
a little more flour. Fold in half
again to form a triangle. Lightly
dust the dough with flour and
roll out into a larger triangle, so
that each side is about 13cm long.
Repeat with the remaining dough.

Heat a heavy-based frying
pan or griddle over a medium
heat. When hot, place one of the
triangles of dough in the pan and
cook for 1–2 minutes, or until
bubbles appear on the surface
and it puffs up. Brush the top with
melted ghee or butter then flip
the bread over, press down with
a spatula so that it cooks evenly,
and cook for a further minute, or
until the bread is golden-brown.
Brush the top with more ghee or
butter, flip it over for a final few
seconds, then remove from the
pan and put on a warm plate
covered by a tea towel while
you cook the rest. Serve warm.

VADAI

Makes about 30

Vadai is a classic South Indian
dish. I saw it being prepared
at the Meenakshi Temple in
Madurai. Traditionally the
patties are made into doughnut-
like shapes with a hole in
the middle, but my version
is easier as you simply drop
them off the spoon into the
hot oil, a bit like falafel.

250g urid dal (black lentils),
washed then soaked in
cold water overnight
1 tsp black peppercorns
½ tsp cumin seeds
40g onion, roughly chopped
2 fresh green chillies, roughly
chopped, with seeds
1½ tsp salt
Vegetable oil, for deep-frying
To serve
Sambar (page 26) and
Coconut chutney (page 304)

Drain the urid dal. Grind
the peppercorns and cumin
seeds to a powder in a spice
grinder (or use a pestle and
mortar). Tip them into a food
processor with all the remaining
ingredients, including the dal,
and blend to a soft paste. It
should be wet enough, but
add a small splash of water
if necessary to help it bind.

Heat the vegetable oil to
180°C in a deep-fat fryer, or
two-thirds fill a deep, sturdy
pan with oil and heat until a
cumin seed dropped in sizzles
vigorously. Carefully drop a
few spoonfuls of the mixture,
about the size of ping-pong
balls, into the hot oil and fry
for 5–6 minutes until crisp
and golden and cooked through.
Remove with a slotted spoon,
drain on kitchen paper and
keep warm in a low oven while
you cook the rest.

RICK'S EVERYDAY PILAU RICE

Serves 4

315g basmati rice
1 tsp vegetable oil
2 cloves
3cm piece of cinnamon stick
1 green cardamom pod, crushed
¼ tsp salt
350ml water

Wash the rice, then soak
for 30 minutes. Heat the
oil in a saucepan and fry the
spices for 30 seconds until
they smell aromatic. Drain
the rice and add it with the
salt; stir a little. Add the water
and bring to the boil, then
cook on a very low heat with
the lid on for 10–12 minutes
until all the water has been
absorbed. Turn out on to a
tray to cool. Reheat in a low
oven when needed.

INGREDIENTS & TECHNIQUES

AJWAIN SEEDS

Also known as carom seeds or bishop's weed seeds, these small brown seeds, related to caraway, have an aniseed and slightly peppery flavour with notes of thyme. They are similar to cumin seeds in appearance. Widely available in Indian stores.

AMCHUR

This pale yellow-brown powder is made from dried green mango and brings a pleasing sourness to dishes such as dals and other curries, particularly in northern Indian dishes. I use it in my recipe for *Aloo dum* (page 86) and it is also an important ingredient in my *Chat masala* (page 303). Buy it ready ground from Indian stores.

ASAFOETIDA (HING)

A pungent, resin-like spice, made from the sap of *Ferula assafoetida.* Can be bought in two forms: as pieces of rock-hard pure resin, which looks a little like amber-coloured glass, or as a powder. The resin has a strong flavour and needs to be used sparingly; the powder is milder so can be used by the pinch. It smells awful in its raw state but once heated in oil or ghee along with other ingredients it adds a background taste reminiscent of fried onions and garlic. Acts as an anti-flatulent, which is one of the reasons it often appears in dal recipes. Keep in an airtight container because of its odour.

BEETROOT POWDER (AND RATAN JOT)

This garish pink-red powder is a natural way to add a vivid red colouring to dishes such as tandoori chicken and fish and butter chicken. Use it sparingly as a little goes a long way. It has a slightly sweet flavour but is used mainly for its colour. Buy it ready-ground from Indian stores.

BENGAL GRAM

Also known as chana dal, this chunky yellow lentil is made from black gram – chickpeas – by first drying then removing the outer skin and splitting them; they look like yellow split peas. They're a good source of fibre and protein and have a nutty, slightly sweet flavour. They're widely used in dishes across India, especially dals (such as my yellow dal on page 106), and also crop up regularly as a deep-fried snack – most notably in Bombay mix or the sweet and tangy potato shreds (lilo chevda) on page 36. They should be soaked in cold water before cooking. In appearance, they are very similar to tur dal, but tur dal is smaller and cooks more quickly.

BLACK SALT (KALA NAMAK)

This pungent salt, smelling strongly of sulphur, can take some getting used to, although once past the shock of the unusual aroma it becomes strangely addictive. Used in my chat masala (on page 303) and in India often sprinkled over nuts or snacks.

CARDAMOM, BLACK AND GREEN

From the same family as ginger come two plants that produce aromatic, oval seed pods, both important in the cooking of India. One produces the green cardamom, and the other the black cardamom. Green cardamom pods have a pale green papery shell inside which lies a cluster of intensely aromatic, small black seeds. These pods can be used whole, or they can be cracked open to release the black seeds which can then be ground to a powder. If they are to be used whole in curries, rice dishes and dals, lightly bruise first so the outer casing cracks, allowing their fragrance and flavour to permeate the dish. They can be removed before serving, but it won't harm you if you end up chewing on one; in fact, in India they are sometimes chewed to freshen the breath. It is possible to buy ready ground cardamom from some suppliers. About 30 pods make 1 teaspoon ground. I sometimes chuck them in whole to save removing the husk and it doesn't seem to make much difference – you just get a bit of the papery husk ground down along with the seeds. Black cardamom pods are quite unlike their green counterpart, being at least twice as large and different in flavour. They are aromatic, with a tinge of camphor, and a smoky flavour that comes from being dried over an open fire; they are often used in rice and dal dishes.

CASSIA BARK

This is a close, and slightly less refined, relative of cinnamon (see page 310) with a more robust flavour and a woodier appearance. Much that is labelled cinnamon is in fact cassia, but cassia is easily recognized as it comes in shards that looks just as you would imagine bark would when peeled off the tree, rather than neatly rolled into quills as cinnamon is. It's sometimes referred to as 'bastard cinnamon'. Ground cassia is reddish brown, not the pale tan of cinnamon.

CHANA DAL

see Bengal gram

CHICKEN

Supermarket free-range chickens have a great deal more fat than Indian chickens, and they don't come close to reproducing the flavour and texture of Indian chicken dishes. For a more authentic taste, try poussins instead. They are bonier, so you need to increase the amount you buy. To replace 1.5kg free-range chicken, use 2.25kg poussin, which is about 5 birds. Or simply aim to serve a poussin per person (or half a poussin per person across a spread of dishes).

CHILLIES, FRESH

When a recipe calls for fresh green chillies, I am referring to the same type throughout the book. These are the fairly mild, large green chillies that vary between about 6cm and 12cm in length, and between a forefinger and thumb in thickness. They're widely available in supermarkets and vegetable shops but seem to vary considerably in their 'hotness'. I've often noticed that in winter in the UK they seem extra mild. Taste a small piece before adding to the dish; if it's very hot then remove the seeds or use a little less; if it's too mild then add more. Fresh red chillies appear once or twice in the book, and these are the same as the green chillies in size.

CHILLIES, KASHMIRI

Used for their deep-red colour and good, but not overpowering, heat, Kashmiri chillies can be bought dried and used whole, broken into pieces or ground to a powder. You can also buy ready ground Kashmiri chilli powder. I use Kashmiri chilli powder throughout the recipes in this book. I find it has an excellent flavour and a reasonable amount of heat, without being uncomfortably hot, and also gives a rich deep-red colour to any dish. If using whole or in pieces, fry with other whole spices in the stage of curry-making known as tempering. The dried chillies can also be soaked and whizzed into a paste, or ground into a powder – simply snip the stalks off then throw the chillies and their seeds into a spice grinder. Eight dried chillies (10g in weight) will yield about 1 tablespoon powder. Making your own Kashmiri powder is often a better option than using one of the highly variable commercial chilli powders, so it's well worth making a large batch (perhaps 100g chillies at a time) and storing in an airtight container for a month or so.

CINNAMON

Cinnamon, as with cassia, is the bark of a laurel-like tree, peeled from the thinner branches and left to dry. Once dry, the curled-up pieces are packed one inside another and cut into short lengths to form the quills, or sticks as we call them. Cinnamon is more expensive than cassia, and the paler the colour, the finer the quality. Powdered cinnamon can be difficult to produce at home so it is best to buy it ready ground, but as with all ground spices, it loses its fragrance quickly.

CLOVES

It is the substance eugenol, which is also present in cinnamon, that gives cloves their distinctive, almost medicinal flavour and aroma. The spice is often used whole in rice dishes and meat curries and is also one of the ingredients in my garam masala on page 303. If used ground, be sparing as they could easily overpower other flavours.

COCONUT FLESH

Use either whole fresh coconut or frozen coconut flesh. Desiccated coconut is not a good substitute unless the recipe specifies it. A small coconut yields about 250g flesh, and a large coconut about 300g. Choose a coconut that feels heavy, and shake it to make sure it is still full of water; which means the flesh is fresh and moist. If you want to save the coconut water from inside, pierce two of the eyes with a thick skewer and drain off the water into a glass; cook with it or drink it. Then whack the shell with a hammer once or twice to crack it open, or throw it on to a concrete floor, and prise out the flesh with a round-bladed knife. There is no need to remove the papery brown skin before preparing grated coconut for the recipes in this book, nor for making coconut milk (see below). Simply break the unpeeled flesh into small cubes, drop it into a food processor and briefly whiz. Excess coconut can be frozen. Packets of finely grated frozen coconut can be bought from most Indian and Asian supermarkets.

COCONUT MILK AND CREAM

Fresh coconut milk is extracted from the flesh. If you leave it to settle for 20 minutes or so, the milk will separate. The thicker opaque liquid that settles on the top is often called the 'cream' and the thinner liquid underneath is the 'milk', but for most of the recipes in this book there is no need to separate the two. Coconut cream can also be bought in small tins or hard blocks; the latter can be grated into curries or dissolved with hot water to make coconut milk.

COCONUT MILK – EXTRACTING

Makes about 200ml

300g fresh coconut blitzed in a food processor (i.e. the flesh from 1 large coconut)
250ml hot water

Combine the coconut flesh and hot water and leave it to stand for about 10 minutes. Then whiz it in a liquidizer or food processor and pour it through a fine sieve (or a muslin-lined sieve) set over a bowl. When most of the liquid has dripped through, press the coconut against the sides of the sieve with your hands to extract every last drop of milk (or twist the muslin around the remaining coconut and squeeze it).

COCONUT OIL

The most heavily saturated of all oils, which in tropical countries remains liquid at room temperature, but in climates like ours solidifies and becomes opaque. Stand the bottle in a jug of hot water until it becomes liquid again, or spoon what you need into a small pan and melt over a low heat. The oil is stable at high temperatures and is used for frying in southern India. While vegetable oil is a good substitute in cooking, coconut oil is an important seasoning for dishes such as thoran on page 72.

CORIANDER SEEDS

These small round seeds are widely used in Indian cuisine and are readily available from supermarkets as well as Indian stores. Their woody, almost sweet flavour complements other spices rather than overpowers, and can be stirred through at the end of cooking in ground form, as well as added whole or ground at the beginning stages of a dish. As with most spices, grinding your own as you need them will give infinitely superior results to buying ready-ground, especially if the recipe calls for them to be toasted and ground.

CUMIN

A widely used spice across India and a major ingredient in garam masala, these small brown seeds of a plant called *Cuminum cyminum* look similar to caraway seeds. They are considered a 'warm' spice and have an earthy aroma; they can be used whole or ground, toasted or untoasted. A lesser-used 'black cumin', *Bunium persicum*, can also be found, which is smaller and sweeter. Confusingly, nigella seeds are sometimes referred to as black cumin.

CURRY LEAVES

Large bunches of these small, slightly pointed, highly aromatic leaves are sold fresh, on the stem, in Asian stores, and are much used, especially in southern India, for their distinctive flavour. They deteriorate quite quickly so I remove the tiny leaves from the stem and store them in an airtight box in the freezer. Don't bother with dried curry leaves – they are as much use as dried parsley.

DAGARFUL (KALPASI OR STONE FLOWER)

This lichen grows on trees and imparts an almost cinnamon-like flavour with slightly bitter undertones. It is not easy to find in the UK, although I have managed to find some from patchapman.co.uk. If you can't find it then use a small extra piece of cinnamon in its place.

DAL

This is the name used for a wide variety of pulses, dried peas, beans and lentils that have been husked and split, as well as for the finished dish. (*See also Chana, Tur and Urid*.)

'DRY' CURRIES

I'm not sure if there is a correct description of what I call a 'dry curry' but what I mean is one where the gravy/sauce/masala has been reduced to such an extent that it is little more than clinging to the meat, fish or vegetables. I'm very fond of these, and examples include the chicken passanda from Lucknow on page 192 and the prawn peera on page 124.

FENNEL SEEDS

The warm, aniseed flavour of these small khaki green seeds adds an important note to many Indian dishes, particularly meat curries, where it balances them with a sort of sweet freshness. They can be used whole or ground; for ground fennel it is best to grind the seeds yourself.

FENUGREEK (METHI) – SEEDS AND LEAVES

As well as the flat, oblong, mustard-coloured seeds, fenugreek is also eaten fresh in India like a herb; it is related to the pea family. The seeds have a pungent, slightly bitter flavour and should be used sparingly, whereas the fresh leaves are milder and can be used in some abundance. At a push you could substitute fresh pea shoots for the leaves, although they won't have the same bitterness. Frozen methi leaves are quite widely available and also very good, I'm told.

FLOUR – CHAPATI

Also sold as 'atta', this finely ground wholewheat flour is used for chapatis and parathas. It is widely available in Indian stores, but as a substitute you can mix equal parts of wholewheat and plain white flour.

FLOUR – CHICKPEA (GRAM OR BESAN)

This pale yellow, finely ground chickpea flour adds a nutty flavour to batters and fritters. It is also used as a thickener and to prevent curdling.

FLOUR – MILLET (BAJRA)

Don't be put off by the grey colour of this finely ground, gluten-free flour; it has an unusual, almost smoky flavour and makes fantastic flatbreads. Because it is gluten free it can be difficult to work with, so some wheat flour is often added to give elasticity to the dough. However, if you want to avoid gluten, it is possible to substitute all millet flour in the recipes for chapatis and millet flatbreads; just add less water to avoid an overly sticky dough. You might also find it easier to press the dough into circles with lightly floured fingers rather than trying to roll it out.

GHEE

This is clarified butter that has been long cooked so its natural sugars slightly caramelize, giving it a delicate nutty flavour. The process of clarifying butter gets rid of the milk solids and so prevents it from going rancid, important in tropical climates. It also makes it an excellent cooking medium, able to withstand high temperatures. It can be bought in tins in Asian stores and some supermarkets. Ordinary clarified butter is a good substitute.

GINGER

This fiery rhizome is available fresh in its root form, or dried and ground to a powder. It is mostly used as a fresh paste in India. You can do this in a mini food processor (see Pastes, page 313), or you can also peel and finely grate it to get a similar result, in which case I find it easier to peel just the part you need, leaving it attached to the rest of the root so you can hold it easily for grating – on a microplane grater is best. Some people use a teaspoon to slip under the thin skin and peel it; a vegetable peeler also works well. It is also cut into fine matchsticks to add texture. In fresh form it should be firm and snap crisply; the flesh should be pale yellow and juicy. It is usually added along with garlic at the cooking stage, or can be used to finish a dish such as the black dal on page 108. It is also one of the main ingredients in my lime and ginger cordial on page 300.

GOAT

see Mutton

INDIAN BAY LEAVES (TEJ PATTA)

Indian bay leaves are not at all like European ones. They have a flavour akin to cinnamon, and therefore it is no use substituting European bay leaves for them. It's perfectly correct to use dried ones; in fact, I never saw them fresh anywhere in India. If you can't get them, leave them out.

JAGGERY

This is the Indian equivalent of the perhaps more familiar palm sugar, but it is made from sugar cane rather than the sap from certain species of palm tree. The cane juice is boiled for hours until it thickens and crystallizes, then it is left to set like fudge; it does, in fact, taste rather like fudge and I find I can't stop eating it straight from the tub. It ranges in colour from pale amber to dark molasses brown, and can be pliable or sometimes so hard that it needs to be grated, pounded or shaved with a sharp knife into shards before use. Store in a well-sealed container, somewhere cool and dry, or it will pick up moisture from its surroundings and become unusable. Light or dark soft brown or muscovado sugar are good substitutes.

KASHMIRI CHILLIES
see Chillies

KOKUM
Made from the rind of a fruit in the mangosteen family. When dried, it is either blackish-red in colour (meaning it's been sun-dried) or deep black (meaning smoke-dried). It has a similar effect in a dish to tamarind; it's sour and performs the same flavour-balancing role as citrus juice or vinegar. Smoke-dried kokum is the one for me, and is the distinctive flavour in many a fish curry in Kerala. It needs to be washed, sliced and soaked in warm water for at least 10 minutes before use.

LAMB
see Mutton

LENTILS
see Tur, Urid

MACE
see Nutmeg

MOOLI
Mooli is the Indian name (and daikon the Japanese), for this large, white, mildly flavoured radish, which is grated as a filling for the parathas on page 306. Go for smaller ones, which have a less bitter flavour and finer texture.

MUNG DAL
There are two types of mung dal. Mung dal chilka is the whole, dried, green mung bean, which has been split, leaving the green husk still in place, and is mainly used in curries. Mung dal is the split and husked bean. It produces a pale yellow pulse that can be soaked and boiled to produce the purée-like dish of the same name, or used in soups or ground into a flour.

MUSTARD OIL
This pungent oil pressed from mustard seeds is popular for cooking, particularly in northern India. It smells quite overpowering straight from the bottle, but mellows in use. It also has good preserving qualities, and so is popular in the making of chutneys and pickles. It also adds an unusual, but important, flavour

to fish curries. Sadly there is some controversy over mustard oil, a suggestion that it is not good for you. I've read a lot about it and there just doesn't seem to me to be any real evidence of its deleterious effects. It's not easy to buy, not in Western stores anyway, but you can find it if you are willing to search.

MUSTARD SEEDS – BLACK AND WHITE/YELLOW
Two main types of mustard seed are used in cooking: black (which is really brown) and white (or yellow). In India, and especially in northern India, mustard seeds are a popular and important spice, where they add heat, piquancy and bitterness. They can be ground into a paste to be stirred into dishes or made into chutneys (see the mustard chutney on page 304). They are also one of the main ingredients of the fish curry on page 178; also commonly used in the spice-tempering stage of many curries and for the tarka that is spooned still hot over dals. When added to hot oil, mustard seeds will spit and sometimes jump out of the pan. Have a lid handy and hold it over the pan if they are spitting too much.

MUTTON
Mutton in India means goat meat, not mature meat from sheep. It's much leaner than lamb and requires long, slow cooking to tenderize it. All the recipes in the book are written for lamb. However, goat meat is becoming much more common. If you're substituting goat meat for lamb, you'll need to cook it for longer than the lamb in the recipes, possibly adding a bit more liquid. (Remember that in India all goat meat recipes call for it to be cooked on the bone; you might decide to do the same.) Here a lot of goat meat is still the byproduct from dairy herds, but goat is increasingly being reared just for the meat. Good-quality meat will come from an animal that is between 6 and 18 months old, although the majority will be 9–12 months old and will yield legs of about 2–2.5kg in weight. The depth of flavour will subtly improve with age without becoming too 'goaty', and as it gets older, despite being more fatty,

it still produces far less fat than a leg of lamb. In fact it has, ounce for ounce, less fat than Western chicken.

NIGELLA SEEDS
Also known as kalonji, or even onion seeds or black cumin (the latter misnomers, as they are neither), nigella seeds are often sprinkled over breads. Deep black in colour, with a slightly bitter flavour a little like mustard seeds, they turn nutty when lightly fried in oil.

NUTMEG AND MACE
These are the only two spices to come from the same tree. Nutmeg is the seed, found inside the nectarine-shaped (though not flavoured) fruit of the tree, and mace is the lacy reddish-coloured coating that covers the seed. Nutmeg should be moist with oil when cut in half with a knife; if it crumbles and is dry it is old and past its best.

OKRA
A vegetable also known as ladies' fingers. The trick is not to overcook it, so that it retains some of its crunchy texture and doesn't become slimy. Snap the tip off one; if it gives a nice 'snap', they are fresh. If it bends, they are old and not worth buying.

ONIONS
Onions and shallots are used widely across India, where they are a pale pink colour and generally smaller and slightly milder than either the brown or red onions in the UK. For eating raw, for example in a salad, I prefer to use red onions or shallots for their sweeter flavour and pleasing colour. But for most of the recipes in this book I found that the standard brown onions work perfectly well. However, and I cannot emphasize this enough, it is essential to cook the onions properly in order to bring out the sweetness and flavour that provides the base of so many of the recipes in this book. See the next entry.

ONIONS – FRYING UNTIL GOLDEN
Fry onions over a moderate heat for at least 10 minutes, and sometimes, if there are more than 2 or 3 onions, for as much as 20 minutes, until they

have softened, turned golden, and are just beginning to darken. It's a matter of cooking off all the water in the onions, after which time they will start to go brown and eventually blacken fairly quickly.

PANEER
Paneer is a very mild, fresh Indian cheese, made by curdling hot milk with lemon juice or diluted vinegar, then letting the whey drain off through a muslin-lined sieve. The remaining solids are lightly pressed until firm enough to hold their shape, after which the cheese can be cut into pieces for cooking. As it comes it is rather bland but it is the perfect vehicle for rich sauces and spice mixes. It is found in the chilling cabinets of larger supermarkets or Indian stores. You can substitute halloumi at a push, although it is much saltier so you need to adjust the quantity of salt in the recipe accordingly.

PASTES
A mini food processor makes light work of turning garlic and ginger, with a splash of water, into pastes, which are used throughout the book. However, for smaller quantities, or if you don't own a mini processor, you can use a microplane grater to finely grate ginger or garlic. Or you can crush the garlic, either by chopping finely with a sharp knife or using a garlic crusher.

PEPPERCORNS
Black peppercorns bring an earthy warmth to dishes and are an important ingredient in India where they are used as an ingredient in their own right, not just as the partner to salt we are more used to. They are a main spice in garam masala as well as chat masala (page 303), and bring the mildly mouth-tingling flavour to my Chettinad chicken (page 216). They can be used whole, coarsely crushed or finely ground; they have much more flavour and warmth if you grind them freshly.

POPPY SEEDS – WHITE
These seeds are harvested from the opium poppy (they do not contain significant amounts of opiates).

They are ground to a paste and used to thicken curries and sauces, adding a nutty flavour. Available from Indian food suppliers. Blue (black) poppy seeds are not a substitute.

RICE – BASMATI
A variety of long-grain rice from northern India, with slightly longer grains than most other types, this rice has the unusual property of becoming longer during cooking rather than fatter. It is revered for its fragrance and delicate flavour, and the fact that it doesn't stick together. Instructions for this type of rice often call for it to be washed to get rid of the excess starch, then soaked in cold water before cooking.

RICE – BOILED BASMATI
Serves 4
I cook my rice for only 10 minutes as I like a very slight firmness to the grain. Simmer for 12–15 minutes if you like a softer texture.

350g long-grain or basmati rice
600ml water

Put the rice into a 20cm heavy-based saucepan and add the water. Quickly bring to the boil, stir once, cover with a tight-fitting lid, reduce the heat to low and cook for 10–15 minutes. Uncover, fluff up the grains with a fork, and serve.

ROSEWATER
Rosewater, a by-product in the making of rose oil, was one of the ingredients left behind by the former Arab rulers of Asia. Its distinctive, perfumed flavour is used in desserts, such as payasam (page 296), but also in Moghul-style savoury dishes like chicken and rosewater biryani (page 214). Be sure to buy rosewater, not the extract, which is far too strong.

SAFFRON
This expensive ingredient is the dried stigma of a specific crocus flower. It is used sparingly because of its price but also because too much can bring an unpleasant, almost medicinal tang to a dish. But used sparingly it adds a seductive, elusive fragrance and striking yellow colour.

For many recipes it should be soaked in a little warm milk or water for a few minutes to release the intense yellow orange colour. In this form it is sprinkled, along with the soaked threads, over the rice in a lamb pulao (page 242) to create a layer of bright yellow rice, as well as in my chicken and rosewater biryani (page 214) and the nimish, sweet yellow rice and other puddings.

SCREWPINE
This is the fragrant essence of the screwpine or pandan leaf. While the whole leaf is used fresh in cooking in India, for us the essence is excellent and well worth tracking down.

SHALLOTS
see Onions

SPICES
Unless you use a lot of spices on a daily basis, buy them in small quantities and store them in well-sealed glass jars, in a cool, dry, dark place. If possible, buy whole seeds, such as coriander, cumin and cardamom, and grind them yourself.

STAR ANISE
A star-shaped seed pod with an aniseed-like flavour, this comes from a small evergreen tree native to China but now grown all over the world. Occasionally added whole in Indian cooking.

TAMARIND
The dried pods of the tamarind tree are used as a souring agent, like kokum (see page 312). The sticky pulp from inside the bean-like pod of the tamarind tree is used to add a slightly sweet tartness to many Indian dishes. Sold in two forms: rectangular blocks of raw pulp, which need to be mixed with warm water and strained to remove the hard black seeds, or in jars and tubs as a concentrated paste that might require diluting. I don't think very much of the stuff in jars, it seems to lack the mouth-puckering sourness that tamarind should bring to a dish. Instead it's worth preparing it yourself.

TAMARIND LIQUID
Take 60g tamarind pulp and put it in a bowl with 120ml just-boiled water.

Leave to soak for 15 minutes, then work the paste with your fingers until it has broken down and the seeds have been released. Strain the slightly syrupy mixture through a fine sieve, rubbing it well against the sides of the sieve to extract as much of the liquid as possible. Discard the fibrous material and seeds left behind. The liquid is ready to use and will keep in the fridge for 24 hours.

TEMPERING WHOLE SPICES

Often a dish in this book will be started with what is called tempering, where whole spices such as cardamom, cinnamon, cloves, coriander and mustard seeds are added to hot oil in a pan and cooked for 30 seconds to a minute to infuse the oil with their flavour. They can often spit when added to hot oil, so take care. Compare with Toasting spices, below.

TOASTING WHOLE SPICES

This is normally done in a dry pan over a medium heat. For perfect results, toast the spices individually, such as for garam masala (page 303), but life is short and I find that if I attend to them carefully I can get away with doing them all together. The idea is to lightly roast the spices until they smell toasted, being careful not to let them burn. After this they can be ground in a spice grinder or using a pestle and mortar. You will notice that whole spices which you toast and grind yourself have a much finer aroma than any you can buy ready-made. Note that you never toast nutmegs.

TODDY VINEGAR

Produced from the sap of the coconut palm, toddy vinegar is made by simply allowing the fermented drink toddy to age, which produces a vinegar rather than a stronger wine. It's mostly used on the west coast of India, particularly in Goa, Karnataka and Kerala. White wine vinegar is a good substitute.

TOMATOES – FRESH VS TINNED/PASSATA

For most of the recipes in the book I have called for tinned tomatoes or passata, simply because most of the year the tomatoes available in the UK don't have anywhere near the flavour and sweetness of those in India. Having said this, in India they always use fresh tomatoes, so if you can get some really ripe, sweet tomatoes then chop them up with skins and seeds and substitute them for tinned. To replace passata, simply blitz the fresh tomatoes in a blender and rub through a sieve, then measure out the required amount.

TUR DAL

Also known as toovar dal, pigeon pea or red gram, this is a dark yellow split pea with a rich, earthy flavour. Used in dals; see tarka dal on page 106 and the Sultan's dal on page 112.

TURMERIC

Another member of the ginger family, fresh turmeric comes in little-finger-sized pieces of root and has bright, carrot-orange flesh. Although powdered turmeric is an adequate substitute, and one that I use throughout the book, it does not match the colour, fragrance and flavour of the fresh stuff. You can find the fresh roots in some Indian groceries; it keeps well in the freezer. Peel off the light brown skin and chop or pound into a paste.

URID

Urid beans are also commonly known as black lentils. In split form they are known as urid dal chilka (with the skin) or urid dal (without the skin). Urid needs soaking in cold water overnight before cooking.

YOGURT

Usually called curd in India, it is slightly tarter and more like a set yogurt than the creamier versions widely available here. I find both natural yogurt or the richer, Greek-style yogurt work well and are less prone to splitting than lower-fat varieties, so I've used these throughout the book. Natural yogurt has a fat content of around 4%, Greek-style is about 10%. Avoid using fat-free in these recipes as this can split.

SUPPLIERS

For fresh ingredients such as curry leaves, fenugreek leaves and even chillies, buy more than you need and keep the surplus, well sealed in plastic tubs, in the freezer, where they will last for at least 3 months and probably come to no harm for up to 6. Store-cupboard ingredients such as flour, rice and dals all have a long shelf-life if well sealed and kept cool and dry. You can also buy frozen items, such as chillies and ready-grated coconut.

www.spicesofindia.co.uk
For most Indian spices and ingredients, including the harder-to-find ones such as fresh fenugreek leaves and fresh curry leaves, kokum, black salt and black cardamoms, millet and chapati flours.

www.theasiancookshop.co.uk
For most Indian cooking ingredients, including fresh daikon, white poppy seeds and black cardamom pods.

www.natco–online.com
For most things Indian: spices, oils, ghee, dals, jaggery, tamarind pulp, rosewater, pickles and chutneys.

www.patchapman.co.uk
For the elusive dagarful as well as silver leaf, black salt and other hard-to-find ingredients.

www.seasonedpioneers.co.uk
For time-saving ground cardamom, garam masala and beetroot powder.

www.herbies.com.au
Very high quality spices from Australia but available in the UK. They sell kokum, aka fish tamarind, used in fish curries in Kerala.

www.goat-meat.co.uk
Free-range goat meat from specially reared Boer goats.

USEFUL EQUIPMENT

KARAHI
In almost all the recipes I've called for a heavy-based pan or karahi. I absolutely swear by a karahi (also called a chati or a kadhi in various parts of India), which is the round-bottomed steel or aluminium pan with loop handles you've probably seen as the serving dish (in its smaller version) in balti houses or other Indian restaurants: see page 139 for a good example. You can buy them very cheaply online from Indian suppliers. I brought one back from India and use it every day. Make sure it's a good thick one so that the heat disperses evenly, with a diameter between 25 and 30cm. A wok is not really the pan for Indian cooking; they are generally too thin and cause slower-cooked dishes to catch and burn.

MICROPLANE GRATER
Not an essential but it makes life easier; it's a good piece of kit for finely grating small quantities of ginger and even garlic.

MINI FOOD PROCESSOR
You may be lucky enough to have a food processor with a smaller bowl for blending or chopping, which is perfect, but if not a mini food processor with a bowl of about 12cm across is the next best thing. Make sure you don't overload it as the motor sometimes can't cope with a heavy quantity of ingredients.

MORTAR AND PESTLE
In India, most households have some sort of mortar and pestle for making curry paste but, realistically, a food processor takes considerably less time. For effective results you would need a mortar and pestle which is at least 10cm deep and 16cm wide (internally). They're quite cheap and look splendid in the kitchen. However, you may prefer just to buy a smaller one for crushing or bruising spices.

SCALES
Digital scales are cheap and I would say indispensable. They are accurate to 2g, 1g or even 0.5g. Especially useful are those that reset to zero so you can weigh each new ingredient as it goes in the bowl.

SPICE GRINDER
Spices are more aromatic if freshly ground, and quite a few recipes in this book also ask you to grind combinations of spices together. Doing this by hand, such as with pestle and mortar, can be hard – it's difficult to get them to a fine enough powder. So I recommend you buy an inexpensive electric coffee mill, which will do the job perfectly.

STEAMER
Some of the recipes in this book require you to use a steamer. A petal steamer placed in a large, deep pan is often sufficient, but in some cases you will need a stackable steamer that provides deep compartments with flat bases on which to place the food.

THERMAL PROBE
This is one of my most valued pieces of equipment. A probe enables you to measure the temperature at the very centre of any piece of meat or fish, ensuring it is perfectly cooked every time. It's also great for checking the temperature of cooking oil, water, and so on. I like the ones called Thermapens, which you can buy online and from good cookware shops.

ACKNOWLEDGEMENTS

Many thanks to: Louisa Carter for taking control of the multitude of information coming in for the recipes, whether it was researchers in India, or snippets from me travelling through Rajasthan or Tamil Nadu and sometimes sending back ideas just scribbled on pieces of paper, and for testing so many of the dishes and making it all coherent.

Liz Bunnell, Arezoo Farahzad and Roopa Gulati for research in India and writing up recipes, and Roopa also for checking through the manuscript for any culinary blunders.

My son Jack and Josh Cooke for testing most of the recipes back at our development kitchen at the Seafood Restaurant so speedily that sometimes I'd email a dish from India and a note would come back 'far too spicy' or 'more salt'.

Muna Reyal, my editorial director, who is delightfully polite but as determined a person as you are ever likely to meet. Not for nothing was this book finished on time and with so many sensible suggestions en route.

Mari Roberts, the copy editor, who I suspect knows more about India than I do, Joe Cottington at Random, and Fiona MacIntyre and Gail Rebuck for again putting so much of Random's resources behind this book.

My PA, Viv Taylor, who managed to fit everything into my diary at a time when I was also writing my memoirs.

I love the look of the book, and thanks first to James Murphy and his assistant Kris for the wonderful photography both of the food and culinary life in India, and Alex Smith for the design; his sensitivity to hues of colour is what one might call Rothkoesque. All of them arrived in Calcutta to take shots as early in the project as I did, and I think it really shows in that both food and locations are inextricably entwined.

Aya Nishimura and Penny Markham, the food and props stylists, have created an immediate look to the food. I don't think I've ever seen the like in a book before. It's richly colourful, rugged, uncompromising, and so makes you want to eat it all. It shows how other talented people can contribute so much to the idea of India as I see it.

And not least the director and producer and my great friend David Pritchard, without whom the book would have been so much the less, because it is filming with an enormously experienced director of food programmes who still absolutely loves the work that turns out great cooking. Not forgetting Arezoo and the boys, too: cameraman Chris Topliss, sound recordist Pete Underwood and, on parts of the trips, researchers Bernard Hall and Chris Denham, boss of Denham Productions.

Lastly thanks to my wife Sas and my stepchildren Zach and Olivia for eating and commenting on so many of these dishes at the numerous curry nights we had in Neutral Bay, Sydney, trying out the recipes on lots of friends.

INDEX

ajwaini fish tikka 179–81
aloo dum 86–9
aloo gobi 90
Amritsari fish 164–5
ande bhujia 34–5
Anglo-Indian cuisine 7, 268
apple chutney 304
apricot & chicken curry with
   potato straws 198–9
asparagus & potato creamy curry,
   with cinnamon, fennel & black
   cardamom 80–1
aubergine, smoky, with tomato,
   ginger & fresh coriander 62–3
avial 91

bainghan ka bharta 62–3
bajra thepla 18
Bali, Sanjiv 232, 260
banana leaf 168–9, 309
beef 227
   bife assado 272–3
   British Raj curry 268–9
   kati rolls 48–51
   vindaloo 266–7
beetroot
   chutney 304
   powder 309
Bengal recipes
   lamb dopiaza 238
   mustardy fish curry 178
   prawn, coconut, green chilli
      & mustard seeds 128–9
berry sour chicken pulao 202–3
bhaji
   my breakfast 60–1
   pau 42–3
bife assado 272–3
biryani
   chicken & rosewater 214–15
   seafood 146–8
Bombay salmon masala curry 171
bread
   & butter pud, Indian-style 282
   chapatis 306, 311
   millet & fenugreek flatbreads 18
   naan 179–81, 306–7
   paratha 23, 306
   Tibetan steamed 22
breakfast bhaji 60–1
butter chicken 210–12
butternut squash
   & spicy lentil soup 26–7
   in sweet tamarind masala 94–5

cabbage
   carrot & coconut dry curry 72–3
   seasonal vegetable curry 66

Calcutta recipes 14–15
   prawn curry & chillies 136
   prawn fritters 40–1
cardamom 80–1, 150, 206–9,
   251–3, 309
   cashew & jaggery kulfi 294–5
   with chicken skewers 220–1
   pistachio & coconut ladoo 290
   shortbread, & mango fool 287–9
carrot
   coconut & cabbage dry curry 72–3
   my breakfast bhaji 60–1
   peas & green beans, quick-fried,
      with coconut 77–9
cashew & jaggery kulfi scented
   with cardamom 294–5
cauliflower 54
   & potato curry 90
   seasonal vegetable curry 66
chai, masala 280, 297–9
chana masala 98–9
chapatis 306, 311
chat masala 303
chicken 188, 309
   & apricot curry with potato
      straws 198–9
   butter 210–12
   Chettinad 216–17
   Mulligatawny soup 31
   passanda 192–3
   pickle 195–7
   pulao 201
   roast, with cinnamon & nutmeg,
      with a pork, cardamom
      & cashew nut stuffing &
      spice-scented gravy 206–9
   Rocky's korma 190–1
   & rosewater biryani 214–15
   skewers, with cardamom 220–1
   sour berry pulao 202–3
   tandoori 194
   vindail 204–5
chickpea curry 98–9
chilli
   garlic relish 304
   Kashmiri 106, 182, 310
   Tibetan sauce 303
   see also green chilli
chingri daab 128–9
chingri malai 126
chutney
   apple 304
   beetroot 304
   coconut 304
   green 303
   mustard 304–5
   & prawn fritters 40–1
   Rick's tomato 305

sweet mango 305
tamarind 304
cinnamon 46–7, 80–1, 150, 206–9, 310
Cochin first-class railway mutton
   curry 254–7
coconut 310
   cabbage & carrot dry curry 72–3
   cardamom & pistachio ladoo 290
   chutney 304
   freshly grated, green chillies &
      mustard seeds with prawns 128–9
   freshly grated, with quick-fried
      green beans, carrots & peas 77–9
   ginger & green chillies with mussel
      masala 154–5
   masala, whole eggs in 104–5
   milk, black cardamom, cinnamon
      & green chilli with fish curry 150
   paste 151–3, 190–1
   prawn curry 126
   spice blends 158–9
   & vegetable stew 91–3
cod
   Bengal mustardy curry 178
   curry 172–3
cordial, lime & ginger 300
courgette & prawn, sautéed 132–5
crab curry, Chettinad 151–3
cucumber & mint raita 304
curry
   Amma's pork 274–5
   Bengal mustardy fish 178
   Bombay salmon masala 171
   British beef Raj 268–9
   Chettinad crab 151–3
   chicken & apricot 198–9
   chickpea 98–9
   Cochin first-class railway
      mutton 254–7
   coconut prawn 126
   cod 172–3
   cooking 9–10
   creamy potato & asparagus 80–1
   defining 7–9
   dry 311
   dry cabbage, carrot & coconut 72–3
   dry prawn, & kokum 124–5
   fish 150
   Kavita's Madras prawn 142
   kidney bean 100
   lamb & sweet potato 239
   lamb & yogurt 235–7
   Madras fish 162–3
   Mr Singh's slow-cooked lamb 251–3
   potato & cauliflower 90
   prawn 136
   Rick's perfect 11
   seasonal vegetable 66

spinach 70
squid 143–5
vegetarian 101–3
white lamb 265
yesterday's fish 176–7

dabi arvi ka salan 239
dal 311
    black 108–9
    mung 312
    sultan's pigeon pea 112
    tur 314
    yellow, with tomato, turmeric
       & fried Kashmiri chillies 106
Dasgupta, Rakhi 126, 178
dhokla, green chilli & turmeric,
    with prawns, curry leaves &
    mustard seeds 24–5
dopiaza, lamb 238
duck 189
    roast 222–3
dumplings, Tibetan steamed 20–1

'eating with your fingers' 10–11
egg
    molee 104–5
    roast, en route to Thekkady 116
    spicy scrambled 34–5
    whole, in coconut masala 104–5
equipment 10, 315

fenugreek 311
    & millet flatbreads 18
fish
    Amritsari 164–5
    Bengal mustardy curry 178
    curry, black cardamom, cinnamon,
      green chilli & coconut milk 150
    fry, garlic, cumin & Kashmiri
      chilli 182
    Madras curry, of snapper,
      tomato & tamarind 162–3
    molee 150
    in a parcel, with green chilli,
      ginger & coriander 160–1
    Pondicherry mackerel fry 183–5
    tandoori, with naan 179–81
    yesterday's, curry 176–7
    see also specific fish
flatbreads, millet & fenugreek 18
flour 311
fool, chilled mango 287–9
fritters, prawn, with chutney
    & kachumber 40–1

garam masala 303
garlic chilli relish 304
ginger 62–3, 154–5, 160–1, 311
    & lime cordial 300
Goan recipes
    beef vindaloo 266–7

bife assado 272–3
    vegetable makhanawala 84–5
gravy, spice-scented 206–9
green beans
    carrots & peas, quick-fried, with
      freshly grated coconut 77–9
    & spicy lentil soup 26–7
green chilli 309–10
    & turmeric dhokla with
      prawns 24–5
    black cardamom, cinnamon,
      coconut milk & fish curry 150
    & Calcuttan prawn curry 136
    coconut, ginger & mussel
      masala 154–5
    coriander, garlic & lamb 247–9
    ginger, coriander & salmon
      parcel 160–1
    mustard seeds, coconut &
      prawns 128–9
    salad 48–51
    tamarind & pork curry 274–5
green chutney 303
Gujurat recipes
    chicken & apricot curry
      with potato straws 198–9
    dhokla with prawns 24–5
    fish in a parcel 160–1
    lamb samosas 45
    my breakfast bhaji 60–1
    spicy scrambled egg 34–5
    sweet & tangy potato
      shreds 36–7

Himachal Pradesh recipes
    butternut squash in sweet
      tamarind masala 94–5
    chicken pickle 195–7
    creamy potato & asparagus
      curry 80–1
    kidney bean curry 100
    morel pulao 117–19
    sweet yellow rice, nuts & dried
      fruit 286
    Tibetan chilli sauce 303
    Tibetan steamed dumplings 20–1

idris yakhni pulao 242–5
Indian cheese 313
    green chilli, yogurt & spinach
      curry 70
    tomato, pepper & vegetarian
      curry 101–3

jaggery 294–5, 312
jalebi 280, 291–3
jungli maas 260–3

kachumber
    chutney & prawn fritters 40–1
    salad 305

kair sangri 66
Kakori kebabs 44
karahi (heavy-based pan) 10, 315
karimeen pollichathu 168–9
Kashmir recipes, rogan josh 258
kasundi 304–5
kati rolls with pickled onion
    & green chilli salad 48–51
kebabs
    Kakori 44
    shami 228–31
kedgeree, hot smoked salmon 170
keema dhai vada 46–7
keema kaleji 247–9
Keralan recipes
    Amma's pork curry 274–5
    cardamom shortbread
      & mango fool 287–9
    chicken skewers 220–1
    Cochin first-class railway
      mutton curry 254–7
    coconut chutney 304
    dry curry of cabbage,
      carrot & coconut 72–3
    duck roast 222–3
    fish curry 150
    flash pickled pineapple
      & onion salad 305
    mussel masala 154–5
    prawn *molee* 138–9
    prawn *peera* 124–5
    Rick's tomato chutney 305
    sambar 26–7
    sea bass pollichathu 168–9
    seafood biryani 146–8
    sweet milk pud & vermicelli 296
    tamarind chutney 304
    vegetable & coconut stew 91–3
    yesterday's fish curry 176–7
kidney bean curry 100
koftas, lamb, in yoghurt,
    with cinnamon & chilli 46–7
kokum 312
    & dry prawn curry 124–5
Kolkatan recipes
    coconut prawn curry 126
    hot smoked salmon kedgeree 170
    kati rolls 48–51
    potato & pea curry 86–9
    whole eggs in coconut
      masala 104–5
korma
    lamb 246
    Rocky's chicken 190–1
kulfi 280
    cashew & jaggery, scented
      with cardamom 294–5

ladoo, coconut, cardamom
    & pistachio 290
lal maas 234

lamb 227
  cutlets, & fennel 232–3
  dopiaza 238
  kofta, in yoghurt, with cinnamon
    & chilli 46–7
  korma 246
  leg of, with red chillies, as cooked
    by hunters in Rajasthan 260–3
  minced liver, fried, with garlic,
    green chilli & coriander 247–9
  Mr Singh's slow-cooked curry,
    with cloves & cardamom 251–3
  pulao 242–5
  red chilli 234
  roast spiced whole leg of,
    from Lucknow 264
  rogan josh 258
  & sweet potato curry in onion
    masala 239
  white curry 265
  & yogurt curry with green
    chillies & sour plums 235–7
lamb mince
  Kakori kebabs 44
  lamb samosas 45
  shami kebabs 228–31
  shepherd's pie as inspired by
    the Madras Club 250
  Tibetan steamed dumplings 20–1
lentil soup, spicy, with squash,
  tomato & green beans 26–7
lilo chevda 36–7
lime & ginger cordial 300
lobster, Mangalore masala 158–9
Lucknow recipes
  chicken passanda 192–3
  Kakori kebabs 44
  lamb & sweet potato curry 239
  lamb pulao 242–5
  nimish 284–5
  roast spiced leg of lamb 264
  Rocky's chicken korma 190–1
  shami kebabs 228–31
  sultan's pigeon pea dal 112

maa ki dal 108–9
mackerel Pondicherry fish fry 183–5
Madras Club 7, 31
  shepherd's pie inspired by 250
Madras curry
  Kavita's prawn 142
  snapper, tomato & tamarind 162–3
makhanawala, vegetable 84–5
mandra 80–1
Mangalore lobster masala 158–9
mango
  chilled fool 287–9
  sweet chutney 305
masala chai 280, 297–9
meen kulambu 172–3
meen masala 171

milk pudding with vermicelli 296
millet & fenugreek flatbreads 18
molee
  fish 150
  prawn 138–9
momos 20–1
monkfish, tandoori, & naan 179–81
mooli 312
  ka paratha 23
morel pulao 117–19
Mulligatawny soup 31
Mumbai recipes
  Bombay salmon masala
    curry 171
  millet & fenugreek flatbread 18
  pau bhaji 42–3
  sour berry chicken pulao 202–3
  squid curry 143–5
mussel masala with coconut,
  ginger & green chillies 154–5
mustard chutney 304–5
mutton 227, 312
  Cochin first-class railway
    curry 254–7

naan 306–7
  & tandoori fish 179–81
nimish 281, 284–5
noodle soup, Tibetan 56
North Indian recipes
  chapatis 306
  cucumber & mint raita 304
  garam masala 303

oil, spiced 195
okra 313
  dry-fried with garlic, cumin
    & garam masala 67–9
onion 9, 313
  browned paste 44
  crisp fried 214–15, 305, 313
  masala, with lamb & sweet
    potato curry 239
  pickled 48–51
  & pineapple salad, flash
    pickled 305
  & potato, spiced roast 306

Pakistan
  bread & butter pudding 282
  chat masala 303
pakoras, vegetable 30
paneer 313
  jalfrezi 101–3
pans 10, 315
paratha 306
  white radish 23
passanda, chicken 192–3
patra ni machi 160–1
pau bhaji 42–3
payasam 296

pea
  green bean & carrot, quick-fried,
    with coconut 77–9
  & potato curry with tomato
    & coriander 86–9
  seasonal vegetable curry 66
pepper
  Indian cheese & tomato with
    veggie curry 101–3
  & tomato sour soup 57–9
pickle, chicken 195–7
pie, shepherd's, Madras Club
  inspired 250
pigeon pea dal, sultan's 112
pineapple & onion salad,
  flash pickled 305
pistachio, coconut & cardamom
  ladoo 290
pollichathu, sea bass, in banana
  leaf 168–9
Pondicherry recipes
  chicken vindail 204–5
  cod curry 172–3
  mackerel fish fry 183–5
  sautéed prawn & courgettes 132–5
poriyal 77–9
pork 227
  Amma's curry, with green chillies
    & tamarind 274–5
  cardamom & cashew nut
    stuffing 206–9
potato
  & asparagus creamy curry,
    with cinnamon, fennel
    & black cardamom 80–1
  & cauliflower curry 90
  my breakfast bhaji 60–1
  & onion, spiced roast 306
  & pea curry with tomato
    & coriander 86–9
  spiced roast 306
  straws 198–9
  sweet & tangy shreds 36–7
prawn
  Bengal mustardy fish curry 178
  coconut curry 126
  curry, with green chillies 136
  curry leaves & mustard seeds,
    with green chilli & turmeric
    dhokla 24–5
  dry curry with kokum 124–5
  with freshly grated coconut, green
    chillies & mustard seeds 128–9
  fritters, with chutney & kachumber
    from Allen Kitchen, Kolkata 40–1
  Kavita's Madras curry 142
  Keralan seafood biryani 146–8
  molee 138–9
  peera 124–5
  sautéed, & courgettes, with salted
    lemon, coriander & basil 132–5